Oxford International Lower Secondary

7

T0369641

English
Student Book

Alison Barber
Rachel Redford

OXFORD

OXFORD
UNIVERSITY PRESS

Great Clarendon Street, Oxford, OX2 6DP, United Kingdom

Oxford University Press is a department of the University of Oxford. It furthers the University's objective of excellence in research, scholarship, and education by publishing worldwide. Oxford is a registered trade mark of Oxford University Press in the UK and in certain other countries.

© Oxford University Press 2023

The moral rights of the authors have been asserted

First published in 2023

All rights reserved. No part of this publication may be reproduced, stored in a retrieval system, or transmitted, in any form or by any means, without the prior permission in writing of Oxford University Press, or as expressly permitted by law, by licence or under terms agreed with the appropriate reprographics rights organization. Enquiries concerning reproduction outside the scope of the above should be sent to the Rights Department, Oxford University Press, at the address above.

You must not circulate this work in any other form and you must impose this same condition on any acquirer

British Library Cataloguing in Publication Data

Data available

ISBN 978-1-38-203599-6

10 9 8 7 6 5 4 3 2

MIX
Paper | Supporting responsible forestry
FSC www.fsc.org FSC® C007785

The manufacturing process conforms to the environmental regulations of the country of origin.

Printed in the UK by Bell and Bain Ltd, Glasgow

Acknowledgements

The publisher and authors would like to thank the following for permission to use photographs and other copyright material:

Cover: Dan Gartman. **Photos: p4(t):** Riccardo Mayer/Shutterstock; **p4(b):** Lebrecht Music & Arts / Alamy Stock Photo; **p5:** Keren Su/China Span / Alamy Stock Photo; **p6:** Neil Cooper / Alamy Stock Photo; **p8:** Chris Jenner/Shutterstock; **p9:** Jonathan ORourke / Alamy Stock Photo; **p10:** makrushka/Shutterstock; **p10:** Styve Reineck/Shutterstock; **p11(l):** Peter Zurek/Shutterstock; **p11(r):** Steve Heap/Shutterstock; **p12:** Michael Robertson / Alamy Stock Photo; **p13:** Nazrul Islam / Alamy Stock Photo; **p14:** Dony Idham Sahadewa/Shutterstock; **p15:** Muhammad Mostafigur Rahman / Alamy Stock Photo; **p17:** World History Archive / Alamy Stock Photo; **p22:** Digital Vision / Getty Images; **p23:** imageBROKER/Kevin Sawford/Getty Images; **p24:** Oleg Kozlov/Shutterstock; **p25:** Bill Bachmann / Alamy Stock Photo; **p26:** FloridaStock/Shutterstock; **p27(t):** Sk Hasan Ali/Shutterstock; **p27(b):** Daniel Prudek/Shutterstock; **p28:** nednapa/Shutterstock; **p29(bkg):** nednapa/Shutterstock; **p29:** Jonas Gratzer/LightRocket via Getty Images; **p30:** Sabelskaya/Shutterstock; **p31(tl):** Anthony Baggett/Dreamstime; **p31(tr):** Bob Pool/Shutterstock; **p31(m):** Paul Banton/Shutterstock; **p31(bl):** robertharding / Alamy Stock Photo; **p31(br):** raclro/iStock/Getty Images; **p32:** SERDTHONGCHAI/Shutterstock; **p33(tl):** Greg Gerla/AGE Fotostock; **p33(tr):** Prisma by Dukas Presseagentur GmbH / Alamy Stock Photo; **p33(b):** Eric Isselee/Shutterstock; **p34:** Hikiray/Shutterstock; **p35(t):** pking4th/Shutterstock; **p35(b):** metamorworks/Shutterstock; **p36:** Digital Vision / Getty Images; **p37:** Sadik Demiroz/Getty Images; **p38:** Noah Sydnor/Shutterstock; **p39:** Artokoloro / Alamy Stock Photo; **p40:** Zdenek Dolezel/Shutterstock; **p41:** Artefact / Alamy Stock Photo; **p43:** Herald and Times/Newsquest Media Group; **p44(t):** Oleskaus/Shutterstock; **p44(b):** Alexander Demyanenko/Shutterstock; **p45:** Peter Tsai Photography / Alamy Stock Photo; **p46:** A_B_C/Shutterstock; **p47:** © Crown copyright. All rights reserved. Dartmoor National Park Authority. 100024842 2009; **p51:** Jack Hong/Shutterstock; **p52:** Photodisc/Getty Images; **p53(t):** Everett Historical/Shutterstock; **p53(b):** melitas/Shutterstock; **p54(t):** Everett Collection / Shutterstock; **p54(b):** iofoto / Shutterstock; **p55(bkg):** REDPIXEL.PL/Shutterstock; **p55(tl):** robertharding / Alamy Stock Photo; **p55(tr):** Three Lions/Getty Images; **p55(bl):** Paul Reeves Photography / Shutterstock; **p55(br):** Angela Hampton Picture Library / Alamy Stock Photo; **p56:** Doulat Khan/Shutterstock; **p58:** Allan Cash Picture Library / Alamy Stock Photo; **p59:** Trevor Smith / Alamy Stock Photo; **p60(l):** avs_lt/Getty Images; **p60(r):** Helen Davies / Alamy Stock Photo; **p61:** Nurlan Kulcha / Alamy Stock Photo; **p62:** Tim Woolcock Photography/Shutterstock; **p63(bkg):** Kaspri/Shutterstock; **p63:** DwaFotografy/Shutterstock; **p64:** Mcmahon/Central Press/Getty Images; **p65:** History and Art Collection / Alamy Stock Photo; **p66:** Twinsterphoto/Shutterstock; **p67:** Sweettoxic/Shutterstock; **p68:** Roger Rosentreter / Shutterstock; **p72:** Gansovsky Vladislav/Shutterstock; **p73(t):** Archive World / Alamy Stock Photo; **p73(b):** Artefact / Alamy Stock Photo; **p74:** Archivart / Alamy Stock Photo; **p75:** Alex DeG/Shutterstock; **p77(t):** Emin Yavuz / Alamy Stock Photo; **p77(b):** REUTERS / Alamy Stock Photo; **p79:** Annett Vauteck/Getty Images; **p80:** 1000 Words/Shutterstock; **p81:** home for heroes/Shutterstock; **p82:** Album / Alamy Stock Photo; **p83:** Leemage/Corbis via Getty Images; **p84:** Photo 12 / Alamy Stock Photo; **p85:** eter Barritt / Alamy Stock Photo; **p86(t):** Uriel Sinai/Getty Images; **p86(b):** Sandra Standbridge / Alamy Stock Photo; **p88:** Chad Ehlers / Alamy Stock Photo; **p89:** antpkr/Shutterstock; **p91:** subman/E+/Getty Images; **p92(bkg):** Ika Hilal/Shutterstock; **p92:** ann_ounce / Alamy Stock Vector; **p93:** lucianospagnolribeiro/Shutterstock; **p94:** Per-Anders Pettersson/Exclusive by Getty Images; **p95(t):** Popova Tetiana/Shutterstock; **p95(b):** Tolimir/Getty Images; **p97:** Mewlish art/Shutterstock; **p98:** wei-ya2019/Shutterstock; **p100(t):** Photodisc / Getty Images; **p100(b):** Berents/Shutterstock; **p101(t):** Pierrette Guertin / Shutterstock; **p101(b):** World History Archive / Alamy Stock Photo; **p102:** Volodymyr Burdiak/Shutterstock; **p103:** Daleen Loest/Shutterstock; **p104:** Mark Trail © 2009 North America Syndicate, Inc. World Rights Reserved; **p105(tl):** Dennis Jacobsen/Shutterstock; **p105(tr):** vladsilver/Shutterstock; **p105(ml):** Digital Vision / Getty Images; **p105(mr):** Digital Vision / Getty Images; **p105(bl):** Amazon-Images / Alamy Stock Photo; **p105(bm):** Ingram / Alamy; **p105(br):** Corbis / Getty Images; **p106:** wim claes/Shutterstock; **p107(bkg):** EsbenOxholm / Shutterstock; **p107(b):** gary yim/Shutterstock; **p108:** Vlada Cech/Shutterstock; **p109(bkg):** Dmod/Shutterstock; **p109(r):** Eduard Kyslynskyy/Shutterstock; **p112:** Saurav022/Shutterstock; **p113:** CreativeAngela/Shutterstock; **p114(t):** blvdone/Shutterstock; **p114(b):** amenic181/Shutterstock; **p116(l):** RGB Ventures / SuperStock / Alamy Stock Photo; **p116(r):** Aerovista Luchtfotografie/Shutterstock; **p117(t):** Index Fototeca / Bridgeman Images; **p117(b):** VVO / Shutterstock; **p118(t):** Universal Images Group via Getty Images; **p118(b):** Paul Severn /Allsport/Getty Images; **p119(t):** imageBROKER / Alamy Stock Photo; **p119(m):** Ernie Janes / Alamy Stock Photo; **p119(b):** Dinodia Photo/Getty Images; **p121:** Ingram Publishing / Alamy Stock Photo; **p122:** The Book Worm / Alamy Stock Photo; **p123:** quisp65 / DigitalVision / Getty Images; **p124:** iStock / Getty Images; **p125(t):** nikos38/Shutterstock; **p125(b):** iStock / Getty Images; **p126:** Giovanni Rinaldi/Shutterstock; **p127:** iStock / Getty Images; **p128:** agsaz/Shutterstock; **p131(t):** Rawpixel.com/Shutterstock; **p131(b):** Joy Brown/Shutterstock; **p132:** Richard Peterson/Shutterstock; **p133:** Graeme Purdy/Istockphoto / Getty Images; **p134:** Atlaspix / Alamy Stock Photo; **p135:** Burben/Shutterstock; **p136:** VasiliyBudarin/Shutterstock; **p137:** Dina Saeed/Shutterstock; **p138:** Lebrecht Music & Arts / Alamy Stock Photo; **p139(bkg):** ann_ounce / Alamy Stock Vector; **p139(tl):** Karin Hildebrand Lau/Shutterstock; **p139(tr):** Thomas M Perkins/Shutterstock; **p139(b):** Nata Bene/Shutterstock; **p139(fgr):** bluestocking/iStock/Getty Images; **p140:** bikeriderlondon/Shutterstock; **p141:** PCH.Vector/Shutterstock; **p145:** Wayne Via/Shutterstock; **p146(t):** Konmac/Shutterstock; **p146(b):** Ulrich Doering / Alamy Stock Photo; **p147(t):** Keith Heaton/Shutterstock; **p147(b):** Here/Shutterstock; **p148:** Evgeniya Pautova/Shutterstock; **p149:** Richard Collingridge; **p150:** photka/Shutterstock; **p151:** Gorynvd/Shutterstock; **p153:** BLUR LIFE 1975/Shutterstock; **p155:** Cholpan/Shutterstock; **p156:** domnitsky/Shutterstock; **p159:** ajt/Shutterstock; **p160(bkg):** makrushka/Shutterstock; **p160(t):** Monika Wisniewska/Shutterstock; **p160(b):** jelenayo/123RF; **p161:** Halfpoint Images/Getty Images; **p162:** HollyHarry/Shutterstock; **p163(t):** Wutthichai Phosri / Shutterstock; **p163(m):** Vlad G/Shutterstock; **p163(b):** Marco Montalti/Shutterstock; **p164:** Cameron Laird/Shutterstock; **p166:** Roman Samborskyi / Alamy Stock Photo; **p168:** Design Pics / Alamy Stock Photo; **p170(t):** alisafarov/Shutterstock; **p170(m):** Olga Popova/Shutterstock; **p170(b):** Kert/Shutterstock; **p170(h):** AntoinetteW/Shutterstock; **p170(i):** Andreas Kraus/Shutterstock **p171:** Marharyta M/Shutterstock; **p172:** Lee Jorgensen / Shutterstock; **p173:** Joseph Sohm/Shutterstock; **p175:** dovrat ostroff/Shutterstock; **p176:** Julie Pla; **p177:** Tim Masters/Shutterstock; **p178:** Ground Picture/Shutterstock; **p181:** Per-Anders Pettersson/Getty Images; **p182:** BLLF/John van Hasselt/Sygma via Getty Images; **p183:** Here/Shutterstock; **p184:** Kristoffer Kvamme Norstad / Shutterstock; **p185(t):** angelo gilardelli / Shutterstock; **p185(b):** Netfalls - Remy Musser/Shutterstock; **p187:** Pictorial Press Ltd / Alamy Stock Photo; **p190:** qvist/Shutterstock; **p191:** Oleg Golovnev / Shutterstock; **p192:** Christopher Wood / Shutterstock; **p191(bkg):** Lukasz Szwaj / Shutterstock.

Artwork by Dan Gartman, Julie Pla, Chayaa Prabhat, Q2A Media, and Oxford University Press.

John Agard: 'I'd Like to Squeeze' from *Get Back Pimple* (Viking Childrens' Books, 1996), copyright © John Agard 1996, reprinted by permission of John Agard c/o Caroline Sheldon Literary Agency Ltd.

Oladipo Agboluaje, **Elizabeth Laird**: Extract from *Oxford Playscripts: The Garbage King* (OUP, 2013). Copyright © Elizabeth Laird.

Shafi Ahmed: 'Bedeh', first published in *The Redbeck Anthology of British South Asian Poetry* edited by Debjani Chatterjee (Redbeck Press, Bradford, 2000), reprinted by permission of the author's heir Hasnat Ahmed.

Judy Allen: extract from *Watching* (Walker Books, 2005), copyright © Judy Allen 2005, reprinted by permission of Walker Books Ltd, London SE11 5HJ.

Peter Allison: Reproduced from *Whatever You Do, Don't Run: True Tales of a Botswana Safari Guide* (Lyons Press, 2014). Copyright © Nicholas Brealey Publishing, 2007. Reproduced by arrangement with Globe Pequot.

Cyril Birch: an extract from *Tales from China* (OUP, 2000). Copyright © Cyril Birch 2000. Reproduced with permission of the Licensor through PLSclear.

Dave Calder: 'Citizen of the World' from *Dolphins Leap Lampposts* (Macmillan, 2002), reprinted by permission of the author.

Amy Choi: 'The Relative Advantages of Learning My Language', first published in *Growing Up Asian in Australia* edited by Alice Pung (Black Inc, 2008), reprinted by permission of the author.

Jane Clarke: 'Finding a Friend', first published in *I Wanna Be Your Mate* edited by Tony Bradman (Bloomsbury, 1999), reprinted by permission of the author.

Kira Cochrane: an extract of 391 words from 'Surviving the tsunami: 'Suddenly the horizon didn't look rightright'' written by Kira Cochrane, Sat 15 Nov 2014. Reprinted by permission from *The Guardian*.

Phil Coleman: extract from the news article – '2021 was a year dominated by hedgehog rescue, says Knoxwood' written by Phil Coleman, published by *News and Star*, 2 Jan 2022.

Deborah Ellis: extract from *Mud City* (OUP, 2003), copyright © Deborah Ellis 2003. Reproduced with permission of the Licensor through PLSclear.

Suzanne Fisher Staples: adapted extract from *Shabanu: Daughter of the Wind* (Walker Books, 2002), text copyright © Suzanne Fisher Staples 1989, reprinted by permission of the publishers, Walker Books Ltd, London SE11 5HJ and Alfred A Knopf, an imprint of Random House Children's Books, a division of Random House, Inc.

Peter Godwin: extract of 88 words from *Mukiwa*. Copyright © Peter Godwin. Reprinted by permission of the author.

Laura Ingalls Wilder: extract from *Little House on the Prairie* (Egmont, 2000), copyright Laura Ingalls Wilder 1953, © renewed 1963 by Roger L MacBride, reprinted by permission of the publishers.

Jackie Kay: 'Bush Fire' from *Red Cherry Red* (Bloomsbury, 2007), reprinted by permission of Bloomsbury Publishing Plc.

Tanya Landman: an extract from *Lightning Strike* (OUP, 2021), Copyright © Tanya Landman 2021. Reproduced with permission of the Licensor through PLSclear.

Karl Mathiesen: extract of 405 words from 'The junk orchestra: making music out of a landfill', *The Guardian*, Karl Mathiesen, Mon 13 Jul 2015. Reprinted by permission from *The Guardian*.

Nick Middleton: extract from *Going to Extremes* (Macmilllan, 2012), copyright © Nick Middleton 2012. Reproduced with permission of the Licensor through PLSclear.

Michael Morpurgo: extract from *Dear Olly* (Collins, 2000), copyright © Michael Morpurgo 2000, and extract from *Toro! Toro!* (Collins, 2001), copyright © Michael Morpurgo 2001, reprinted by permission of HarperCollins Publishers Ltd.

Lupenga Mphande: poem 'Why the Old Woman Limps' from *The Heinemann Book of African Poetry in English* edited by Adewale Maja-Pearce (Heinemann, 1990). Copyright © 1990 Lupenga Mphande. Used by permission from the author.

Andy Mulligan: extract from 'Trash' (OUP, 2012) Copyright © Andy Mulligan. Reproduced with permission of the Licensor through PLSclear.

Linda Sue Park: extract from *A Single Shard* (OUP, 2001), copyright © Linda Sue Park 2001.

Bill Paterson: extract from *Tales from the Back Green* (Hodder & Stoughton, 2008), copyright © Bill Paterson 2008, reprinted by permission of the publishers and David Godwin Associates Ltd.

Naomi Shihab Nye: excerpt from *19 Varieties of Gazelle*. Text copyright © 2002 Naomi Shihab Nye. Used by permission of HarperCollins Publishers. Poems 'Not My Problem' and 'Trash Talk' from the book *Cast Away: Poems of Our Time* (HarperCollins, 2020).

Repair Café: extract from webpage – About https://www.repaircafe.org/en/about/. Copyright 2022 Repair Café. Used by permission.

UN Environment Agency: extract from the article 'Celebrity chefs serve up free meals from discarded food' by UN Environment Agency, Copyright © 2015 United Nations. Reprinted with the permission of the United Nations.

Rachel Redford: 'Carisbrooke Castle, Isle of Wight'; retelling of the African folk tale 'Something in the Air'; 'The Man-eating Tiger'; retelling/translation of Pliny the Younger's account of the eruption of Mount Vesuvius; all written for the first edition and reused by permission of the author.

Any third-party use of this material, outside this publication, is prohibited. Interested parties should apply to the copyright holders indicated in each case.

Every effort has been made to contact copyright holders of material reproduced in this book. Any omissions will be rectified in subsequent printings if notice is given to the publisher.

Contents

1 Water, water

How do we use water?

> ❛ Water, water, everywhere,
> Nor any drop to drink. ❜
>
> From 'The Rime of the Ancient Mariner'
> by SAMUEL TAYLOR COLERIDGE

Talk about ...

- Why is water important to us?
- Discuss the ways you use water each day.
- Look at the quotation on the left. How can there be water everywhere that isn't drinkable?

The quotation by Samuel Taylor Coleridge above comes from a poem about a dramatic sea voyage. Before reaching calmer waters, the ship is swept into the stormy seas of the Antarctic.

What do you think it would be like to be on the ship shown in the wood engraving on the right? What would you be able to hear, see, taste and smell?

In this unit, you will learn about how people need, use and feel differently about water around the world.

Wood engraving by Gustave Doré, 1876. It shows the storm described in Coleridge's poem.

A story about a desert family

In the following text, a 12-year-old girl, Shabanu, describes her morning ritual. She lives with her family and their camels in the Cholistan Desert in Pakistan. Water is extremely precious to them. When their water source dries up, they move on to another part of the desert.

- Read a wide range of texts and express opinions
- Think about where words come from

Word origins

Some of the Urdu names in this story have similar translations to some English names.

Shabanu (n), comes from the eighth Islamic month, 'Shaaban'

Phulan (n), meaning 'flower'

Mithoo (n), affectionate name meaning 'sweet'

Morning in the desert

The sky is pearl-grey when I awake. My sister Phulan pushes me out of bed. Yawning and rubbing my eyes, I tie a piece of soap into the corner of my chador. I pick up two earthen pots and a padded ring to balance one pot on my head. The other
5   fits under my arm, balanced on my hip. My camel, Mithoo, and I set off for the water hole, the toba. Mithoo's small brass bell jingles cheerfully as he moves his head, impatient for me to fold back the reed door which leads from our courtyard to the outside. I make Mithoo carry the empty goatskin to the toba.

10   At the toba I look out over our dwindling water supply. We probably have a month, perhaps three weeks, before the water disappears. The monsoon will not begin for another two months. Then will be the time for flowers, mushrooms, weddings and water, but not now. Two-toed camel footprints are baked into the
15   shiny clay at the outer edges of the toba. I lift my skirt with one

Glossary

chador shawl or veil worn to cover head and shoulders
toba water hole

hand, and the mud squirts between my toes as I enter the water. I push aside the green scum that floats just under the surface and place the edge of my chador over the mouth of the water pot to filter out impurities. I take the filled pot to the bathing rock at the

20 edge of the toba and lift my tunic over my head. I throw my hair forward and pour water over it.

The sun edges over the horizon. I can feel its heat on my back and shoulders as the water trickles over my scalp. I rub the soap into my hair. I squeeze my eyes shut, letting the soapy

25 water drain down my shoulders and neck, rubbing into my skin before rinsing off to preserve every drop. Mama used to bath my sister and me with a single cup of water when we were small.

The sun is extremely hot as I walk back. Over the next week

30 we watch our water dwindle yet further. In the heat of the afternoons, before the daily wind and dust arrive, we dry herbs. As the precious water slips away with the hot desert wind, we also make our preparations for leaving the toba and moving on.

From *Shabanu: Daughter of the Wind* by SUZANNE FISHER STAPLES

Pakistani women carrying water jars in the desert

- Use clues in a story to answer questions
- Write organized, structured texts
- Write grammatically correct sentences

Comprehension

1 What does Shabanu take with her to the water hole?
2 How does Shabanu manage to carry two pots to the water hole?
3 How will the monsoon change the family's life?
4 How does Shabanu make sure that the water she collects in her pot is clean?
5 Why do you think the water level is so low?

1 Shabanu describes the sky in the morning as 'pearl-grey'. (line 1) Describe the picture this creates in your head.
2 What tells you that the water is not very clean? (paragraph 2)
3 What descriptive words are used in paragraph 4 to emphasize the conditions?

1 Suggest some ideas that would make Shabanu's life easier.

Is your way of life the same or different?

In the story *Shabanu: Daughter of the Wind,* water is a luxury for Shabanu and her family and they use as little as possible. When Shabanu was young, her mother washed the children using just one cupful! How is your day similar to Shabanu's day? How is it different?

- Create a Venn diagram, like the one below, that compares Shabanu's way of life to your own. You may have used Venn diagrams in mathematics, but you can also use them to arrange ideas.
- Write three paragraphs in which you compare Shabanu's life with your own. The Venn diagram will help you to decide what to put in each paragraph.

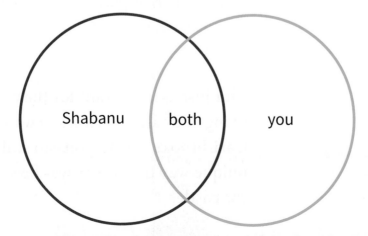

Language tip
Notice that this story is written in the **present tense**. To change it to the **past tense**, use the simple past tense form of the verb.

Present tense: 'I <u>make</u> Mithoo carry the empty goatskin.'

Past tense: 'I <u>made</u> Mithoo carry the empty goatskin.'

Stretch zone

When you finish reading the story, go back and review words you didn't understand. Examine each of the words in its context in the sentence. Then check the definitions in a dictionary and record the meanings.

How did people get water in the past?

For thousands of years, people have faced the problem of getting water up from under the ground.

In Britain, there are a lot of old castles and fortifications. Long ago, people lived inside these walls so a source of water was essential. Today, the castles are attractive places for visitors.

Carisbrooke Castle was built in the Middle Ages on the Isle of Wight, an island off the south coast of Britain. The following leaflet is about the donkey-powered well there.

Glossary

Middle Ages period of European history from around 500 to 1500 CE

strongholds fortified places for defence

treadwheel wheel that is kept moving by an animal or person walking on it

The gatehouse entrance to Carisbrooke Castle

Carisbrooke Castle, Isle of Wight

Have a great day out and learn about the island's history!

Carisbrooke Castle can be found right in the middle of the Isle of Wight. The main castle walls that stand today were built by Norman rulers in the eleventh and twelfth centuries.

The hill the castle is on was used as a site for several previous strongholds. A hill is a great place to build a castle because it can be defended from enemy attack.

But just as important for the people living in a castle is access to water! At Carisbrooke Castle, you can still see the unique way that water was brought into the castle.

- Read a variety of texts and consider their features

Talk about ...

- Does the leaflet make you think you would like to go there? Why? Or why not?
- Both paragraphs and bullet points are used to organize information in the leaflet. Discuss which style you think is best and why.
- How could the leaflet be improved?

Language tip

The **passive voice** is useful when you want to describe how something was done to someone or something, without saying who did it.

For example: 'Carisbrooke Castle <u>was built</u> in the Middle Ages.'

Come and see the only donkey-powered well in Britain!

- The well at Carisbrooke Castle was dug in 1136 when the original water source dried up.
- A wooden bucket was used to collect water from the well, which is 49 metres deep.
- A well-house and treadwheel were built in 1291 and donkey power was introduced to the castle.
- In 1587, the treadwheel was rebuilt by later island rulers. You can see one of the six castle donkeys working the treadwheel today!

Water being drawn from the well, just as it was many centuries ago

- Write a non-fiction leaflet using suitable vocabulary

Design a leaflet

Use the information below from a website about the water wheels in Hama, Syria to plan and design a leaflet about them. Do some additional research to add further detail to your leaflet.

- Look at leaflets of places of interest in the country where you live for inspiration. With a partner, draft your own ideas for a leaflet to encourage people to come and see the amazing water wheels.
- When you have finished, compare your leaflet plan with those of others in your class. Which features do you think work best?
- Display your final, colourful version in the classroom.

Glossary

aqueduct artificial channel for carrying water

irrigate bring water through artifical channels to supplement rainfall and support more intensive farming practices

---

The water wheels (*norias*) of Hama, Syria

- Hama is about 140 kilometres from Aleppo in Syria.
- Settlements in Hama go back to the Bronze Age and the Iron Age.
- Hama's water wheels (*norias*) are up to 20 metres in diameter, the height of a five-storey building.
- *Norias* have been in Hama since at least the fifth century.
- 17 of the 30 *norias* built in the thirteenth century still survive today.
- The wheels bring up water from the Orontes River, which is lower than the land.
- *Norias* are driven by the current of the water acting upon the paddles, and they require no other form of power to keep them going.
- Water fills and drives the wooden boxes that empty into aqueducts at the top of the wheel's rotation.
- Wheels were used to supply the town with water and for irrigating crops in the surrounding farmland.

- Although no longer applied to practical use, the wheels still turn in spring and summer for the benefit of tourists.
- Creaking and groaning as they bring up the water, they are a wonderful sight and a reminder of Syria's fascinating past.

- Read a range of texts and express opinions
- Give own opinions clearly and confidently

Life on the water

When you were discussing ways you use water at the start of the unit, did anyone think of using water as a place to live? Look at the pictures below. What would life be like living in these places? Share your opinions in small groups.

Traditional bamboo house in one of the floating villages of Inle Lake, Myanmar

Floating village on Tonlé Sap Lake, Cambodia

On the next page, you will read a story about a group of nomadic people who live and work on their boats in Bangladesh. Look at the map to see just how large the river delta is in Bangladesh. The group of people in this story are known as *Bedeh* (the name they have chosen for their clan), or 'river gypsies' to the local people.

Glossary

nomadic moving from one place to another, instead of living in one place

delta land formed at the mouth of a river by the mud and sand deposited by water

clan large, extended family

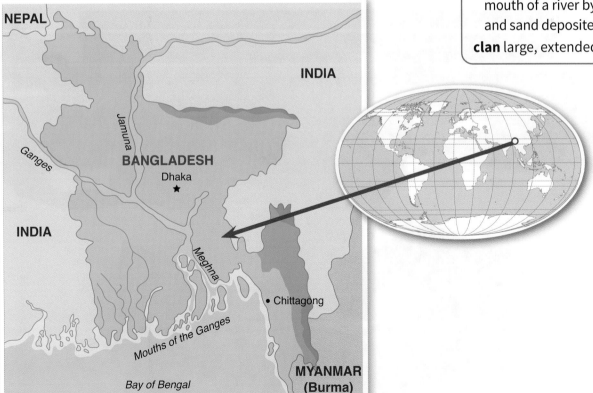

Map of Bangladesh, showing its large river system

- Read a range of texts and express opinions

A story about cobras

The *Bedeh* clan are renowned for their skills in handling snakes. The writer Nick Middleton met them on his travels and the following text recalls an occasion when these skills were put to good use.

The river gypsies

My friend, Babu, and I stood amongst the crowd watching the river gypsies with their snakes. Beside them were several wooden boxes in which they kept their snakes. From one of these boxes one of the gypsies had produced half a dozen small snakes
5 which were winding themselves round his wrists like bright green bangles. The other gypsy, who wore a purple headscarf tied round his forehead, was dangling his hands in front of a hooded cobra which was rising up from another box. The crowd watched in horror and delight.

10 Suddenly there was a small commotion in the crowd and an old man came forward and spoke to the river gypsies, who immediately began to coax their snakes back into their boxes.

"The old man has a snake in his house," Babu explained to me.

Glossary

cobra type of poisonous snake found in Asia and Africa
coax persuade someone or something gently or patiently

- Read a range of texts and express opinions

15 The crowd followed the river gypsies to the old man's house, the backyard of which sloped down to the flooded fields. One of the river men gathered some earth from the entrance and rubbed it between his hands. He smelt it and gave it to his colleague in the purple headscarf to do the same.

20 "If the earth smells of fish, then the men know there's a snake inside," Babu whispered to me.

The river gypsies entered the main room which had a bed on one side, and a neat row of cooking pots hung above a sideboard on the other. The owner of the house, evidently pleased to see a foreigner, beckoned me into his bedroom and
25 pointed to the bed. This was the safest place from which to watch the proceedings. Suddenly there was a commotion beneath the sideboard and the river gypsy with the purple headscarf darted underneath it. He emerged holding a full-sized cobra as long as his arm. The snake hissed as the river
30 gypsy expertly twisted his arm to prevent the snake from striking him. The crowd let out a collective gasp as he began to force the cobra into one of his boxes.

But the show was not over yet. The other river gypsy had his head beneath the bed on which I was cowering. He emerged
35 in a flash holding a second cobra, just as long as the first.

"Husband and wife!" cried Babu. "Cobras are faithful partners. They always travel together!"

From Going to Extremes *by* NICK MIDDLETON

Language tip

Writing **direct speech** involves putting quotation marks around the words that are said.

For example:

"The old man has a snake in his house," Babu explained to me.

Indirect speech involves changing the sentence to the past tense, adding the word 'that' and changing the pronoun.

For example:

Babu explained to me that his friend needed the snake catchers.

- Explain how language features create effects
- Write from a character's point of view
- Use suitable vocabulary
- Use punctuation correctly
- Contribute to discussions and share own ideas

Comprehension

A

1 What caused the small commotion in the crowd?

2 Why do you think the river gypsies immediately started to put their snakes back in their boxes?

3 Why didn't the snake from underneath the sideboard bite the man?

4 How did the river gypsies know there would be a second cobra in the house?

B

1 What simile is used in the first paragraph? What picture does this create?

2 Why has the writer used the words 'horror and delight' to describe the way the crowd was feeling? (line 9)

3 What word for 'a disturbance' is used twice?

4 What do you think the people in the crowd were thinking when they 'let out a collective gasp'? (line 31)

C

1 How safe do you think the bed was to watch the river gypsies in the house? Give reasons for your answer.

2 What do you think the river gypsies will do with the cobras they captured?

3 Discuss what action you would take if you found a cobra in or near your house.

There's a snake in my house!

'The river gypsies' is written in the first person, which is the writer's point of view. The 'I' is the writer himself, and he is retelling the events as he remembers them. He often uses the simple past tense to describe what happened. The text presents things in a chronological order. (That means that things are told in the order in which they happen.)

Now pretend that you are the old man who had the snakes taken from his home. You meet a neighbour who was away when the river gypsies came, and she asks you to explain what happened.

- Write an account from the old man's perspective. Make it sound very exciting.
- Remember to write in the first person and mainly use the past tense – but watch out for any irregular verbs.

You will need to make use of the details from the text, including what Babu says.

Can you make this poem into a picture?

The following poem was written by Shafi Ahmed, who was born in Bangladesh in 1937. The first-person 'I' in this poem is a member of the *Bedeh* clan in Bangladesh.

Poetry often creates images in your head. After you have read or listened to the poem, choose some lines from 'Bedeh'. Illustrate the lines you have chosen using pictures and sketches. You may choose to make the words part of your illustration.

Bedeh

This is the name of my clan.
I am a water-gypsy
on the turbulent rivers of Bangladesh.
My boat is home
5 to me, my wife, and our children.

I have some knowledge of words
and wild herbs.
I treat snake-bites, drive out evil spirits,
and attempt things which others dare not.
10 Tigers, robbers, snakes, demons, storms
all seem to leave me alone!

My needs are small and simple.
They are easily met
from day to day, from hand to mouth,
15 from one river settlement
to the next.

Sometimes in fine weather
I row out to the river's end.
I meet many ships at the anchorage.
20 The crew exchanges foodstuffs,
old clothes, newspapers,
empty cans and bottles
with my beads, bangles,
bamboo-toys and seashells.

25 Once I had a chance to board
an English ship.
I marvelled at the ocean-going craft.

- Identify and discuss ideas in poems
- Discuss how language features create effects

But the Captain, he marvelled: at me,
at the size of my boat,
30 at how we had survived, at how we live!
He wrote down our names,
and other things in his notebook.
He said, one day he would write about us.

I cannot imagine
35 Why anyone would want
To do that!

SHAFI AHMED

What do you think would be the biggest disadvantages of living on a boat? What advantages are there?

Comprehension

1 Apart from treating snake-bites, what does the river gypsy do?

2 What does the river gypsy do when the weather is good?

3 What is it about the river gypsy that causes the Captain to marvel at him?

4 What is the Captain doing with the notes in his book?

1 The river gypsy describes the rivers of Bangladesh as 'turbulent'. In what ways would turbulent rivers make life difficult for the river gypsy? (line 3)

2 The river gypsy lives a 'hand-to-mouth' existence. What does this expression mean? (line 14)

1 What gives the reader the impression that the river gypsy has a humble opinion of himself?

How can water make us feel?

While you have been thinking about the ways we use water, have you considered going to the beach or doing water sports? Can water be exciting, relaxing, or both?

The painting on the next page is by the French artist Edgar Degas, and it was painted in the nineteenth century. Degas liked to paint ordinary people enjoying their free time. In this image, a woman combs the hair of a young girl, who has fallen asleep in the sun, listening to the sound of the waves.

Painting a scene with words

In this painting, Degas uses paint instead of words to describe the beach scene and create an effect.

Now describe the scene on the beach, including the characters, to a partner using descriptive language. How is the effect created by words different to the effect of the painting?

- Explore how setting and character are developed
- Explain how language features create effects
- Contribute to discussions and share own ideas

Beach Scene by Edgar Degas, painted between 1869–70

Talk about ...

- As a group, tell the story of what is happening in the painting.
- Why do you think the woman and the young girl have come to the seaside today?
- What do you think the people in the painting might be thinking and feeling?

 Stretch zone

How would you describe the colour palette the artist uses? Write notes on how it affects the mood and atmosphere of the painting.

Is it true that 'a picture is worth a thousand words'?

Life on a country farm in the US

This is the story of a family of settlers who travelled to the western part of America in the nineteenth century before it was part of the United States. Many families joined 'wagon trains' in search of wealth, excitement and a better life. Here the father of the family, Pa (or Mr Ingalls) finds trouble while digging a well. His neighbour, Mr Scott, is helping him dig the well.

- Read a range of texts and express opinions
- Explore how setting and character are developed

Fresh water to drink

Every morning, before Pa would let Mr Scott go down the rope, he set a candle in a bucket and lighted it and lowered it to the bottom. Once Laura peeped over the edge and she saw the candle brightly burning, far down in the dark hole in
5 the ground.

Then Pa would say, "Seems to be all right," and he would pull up the bucket and blow out the candle.

"That's all foolishness, Ingalls," Mr Scott said. "The well was all right yesterday."

10 "You can't ever tell," Pa replied. "Better safe than sorry."

Laura did not know what danger Pa was looking for by that candle-light. She did not ask, because Pa and Mr Scott were busy. She meant to ask later, but she forgot.

One morning Mr Scott came while Pa was eating breakfast.
15 They heard him shout: "Hi, Ingalls! It's sun-up. Let's go!" Pa drank his coffee and went out.

The windlass began to creak and Pa began to whistle. Laura and Mary were washing the dishes and Ma was making the big bed, when Pa's whistling stopped. They heard him say,
20 "Scott!" He shouted, "Scott! Scott!" Then he called: "Caroline! Come quick!"

Ma ran out of the house. Laura ran after her.

"Scott's fainted, or something, down there," Pa said. "I've got to go down after him."

25 "Did you send down the candle?" Ma asked.

Glossary

windlass tool for lifting heavy weights
Pa Father
Ma Mother

- Read a range of texts and express opinions
- Explore how setting and character are developed

"No. I thought he had. I asked him if it was all right, and he said it was." Pa cut the empty bucket off the rope and tied the rope firmly to the windlass. "Charles, you can't. You mustn't," Ma said.

30 "Caroline, I've got to."

"You can't. Oh, Charles, no!"

"I'll make it all right. I won't breathe till I get out. We can't let him die down there"

[...] "Charles, if I can't pull you up – if you keel over down

35 there and I can't pull you up –"

"Caroline, I've got to," Pa said. He swung into the well. His head slid out of sight, down the rope.

Ma crouched and shaded her eyes, staring down into the well.

All over the prairie meadowlarks were rising, singing, flying

40 straight up into the sky. The wind was blowing warmer, but Laura was cold.

Suddenly Ma jumped up and seized the handle of the windlass. She tugged at it with all her might. The rope strained and the windlass creaked. Laura thought that Pa had keeled over, down

45 in the dark bottom of the well, and Ma couldn't pull him up. But the windlass turned a little, and then a little more.

Pa's hand came up, holding to the rope. His other hand reached above it and took hold of the rope. Then Pa's head came up. His arm held on to the windlass. Then somehow he got to the

50 ground and sat there. [...]

Glossary

keel over fall over, collapse

- Read a range of texts and express opinions
- Explore how setting and character are developed

The rope slowly wound itself up, and the bucket came up out of the well, and tied to the bucket and the rope was Mr Scott. His arms and legs and his head hung and wobbled, his mouth was partly open and his eyes half shut. [...]

55 "He's breathing," Pa said. "He'll be all right, in the air. I'm all right, Caroline. I'm plumb tuckered out, that's all." [...]

That was a terrible day.

"I don't want a well," Ma sobbed. "It isn't worth it. I won't have you running such risks!"

60 Mr Scott had breathed a kind of gas that stays deep in the ground. It stays at the bottom of wells because it is heavier than the air. It cannot be seen or smelled, but no one can breathe it very long and live. Pa had gone down into that gas to tie Mr Scott to the rope so that he could be pulled up out of the gas.

65 When Mr Scott was able, he went home. Before he went he said to Pa: "You were right about that candle business, Ingalls. I thought it was all foolishness and I would not bother with it, but I've found out my mistake."

"Well," said Pa, "where a light can't live, I know I can't. And
70 I like to be safe when I can be. But all's well that ends well."

Pa rested awhile. He had breathed a little of the gas and he felt like resting. But that afternoon he unravelled a thread from a tow sack, and he took a little powder from his powder-horn. He tied the powder in a piece of cloth with one end of the tow
75 string in the powder.

"Come along, Laura," he said, "and I'll show you something."

They went to the well. Pa lighted the end of the string and waited until the spark was crawling quickly along it. Then he dropped the little bundle into the well.

80 In a minute they heard a muffled bang! and a puff of smoke came out of the well. "That will bring the gas," Pa said.

When the smoke was all gone, he let Laura light the candle and stand beside him while he let it down. All the way down in the dark hole the little candle kept on burning like a star. [...]

85   One day when Pa was digging, a loud shout came echoing up. Ma ran out of the house and Laura ran to the well. "Pull, Scott! Pull!" Pa yelled. A swishing, gurgling sound echoed down there. Mr Scott turned the windlass as fast as he could, and Pa came up climbing hand over hand up the rope. [...]

90   In a little while the well was almost full of water. A circle of blue sky lay not far down in the ground, and when Laura looked at it, a little girl's head looked up at her. When she waved her hand, a hand on the water's surface waved, too.

   The water was clear and cold and good. Laura thought she
95   had never tasted anything so good as those long, cold drinks of water. Pa hauled no more stale, warm water from the creek. He built a solid platform over the well, and a heavy cover for the hole that let the water-bucket through. Laura must never touch that cover. But whenever she or Mary was thirsty, Ma
100   lifted the cover and drew a dripping bucket of cold, fresh water from that well.

From *Little House on the Prairie* by LAURA INGALLS WILDER

Comprehension

 A

1 Why do you think Pa needs help digging his well?

2 What danger is Pa looking for by lowering his candle into the well?

3 Why doesn't Ma want Pa to go into the well after Mr Scott?

 B

1 What effect is created by the short sentences in lines 28 to 31?

   "Charles, you can't. You mustn't," Ma said.

   "Caroline, I've got to."

   "You can't. Oh, Charles, no!"

2 Figurative language gives extra meaning to a story. Find an example of a simile and a metaphor in lines 77 to 84, explaining how these add to the picture created in your head.

 C

1 Discuss how Laura's emotions change as the story progresses.

 Stretch zone

List any words you didn't understand from the extract. Look the words up in a dictionary.

2 Climate

How are animals affected by changes in climate?

> ‘Scientists predict that if current trends continue, the polar bear population faces a high risk of extinction by the end of the twenty-first century.’
>
> YOUNG PEOPLE'S TRUST FOR THE ENVIRONMENT, 2022

Talk about ...
- What do you know about climate change?
- How might the situation of the polar bears be connected with climate change?
- Discuss any recent news stories you have heard or read about the effects of climate change.

Word origins

ecology (n), the prefix *eco* comes from the Greek word *oikos*, meaning 'house', and the suffix *logy* comes from the Greek word *logos*, meaning 'study'

Related words:
- ecologist
- ecological
- ecosystem

In this unit, you will consider how dependent all living things are on their climate and environment. Look at the 'Word origins' box to the right. Scientists who study and research the relationship between animals, plants and their environment are called 'ecologists'. Considering the word's origin, do you think this is a good name for them?

- Read a non-fiction text and discuss its features
- Summarize a text and understand its purpose

Hedgehogs in danger

The news article below is about hedgehogs, which are now classified as 'vulnerable to extinction' in Britain. A journalist explains how more and more hedgehogs are struggling to find food.

2021 was a year dominated by hedgehog rescue, says Knoxwood

A NORTH Cumbrian [North of England] wildlife sanctuary is rescuing an increasing number of hedgehogs, with some shocked out of hibernation by
5 **unseasonably warm weather and hunger.**

For more than 30 years, the Knoxwood Wildlife Rescue Trust has helped orphaned and injured animals. But over the last year, amid repeated headlines about climate change and environmental crisis, the sanctuary,
10 near Wigton, has witnessed surging numbers of struggling hedgehogs. "Hedgehogs were the main creature brought to us last year – small, dehydrated ones, often disturbed, or picked up by dogs," said Emma Scott, whose father George founded the sanctuary.
15 "The number we've had in runs into several hundred. They're quite specialized creatures, and don't adapt well and they're very dependent on the weather."

"Ideally, they need damp, warm summers and then cold in the winter as they hibernate. But because the
20 summer season's been either ridiculously dry or completely flooded, they've struggled to find food."

"There seem to be pockets of them in parts of Cumbria where they're doing well – the small village hedgehogs, where people look out for them and help them out.
25 But they're not doing so well in other areas. I think hedgehogs are going to depend more and more on people helping them out."

Emma rejects a suggestion that people should avoid 'interfering' to help struggling hedgehogs. "Their
30 environment's changed so much," she said. "And that's down to us, so we've already interfered and now these little guys are struggling. Helping out will hopefully keep them going. There's a range of reasons they are coming to us: the usual accidents and incidents as well
35 as hedgehog-specific ailments. They suffer terribly with lungworm, picked up from cattle. They also get

hypothermia really easily because they're essentially bald underneath their quills. They get a good soaking and end up chilled."

Gardeners sometimes can inadvertently destroy 40 hedgehog habitats – for example, by strimming rough ground or demolishing a shed. Hedgehogs normally hibernate between October and April. "But we've been getting hedgehogs in all through December," said Emma. "Usually, the up-to-weight, healthy tend to sleep 45 through but any which are not in peak condition when they go into hibernation wake up and poddle about, looking for food; and then they get caught out in rain. We had a lady bring one in recently which she found swimming across her garden because she'd been flooded 50 out and this little guy was washed out of his home."

She gave this advice to people wanting to help Cumbria's struggling hedgehogs:

- Check for hedgehog nests before doing any disruptive garden work   55
- Support them with dry cat food and a saucer of water (not milk)
- Provide garden access points (such as in a fence) so hedgehogs can roam freely
- And consider buying or making a hedgehog house. 60

NEWS AND STAR, JANUARY 2022

'Hedgehog Highways' like this one enable the animals to roam from garden to garden

- Use clues in a text to answer questions
- Understand the difference between facts and opinions
- Understand how texts are structured and organized
- Carry out research
- Plan and proofread writing

Comprehension

1 What problems are the hedgehogs having because of the climate?
2 What evidence is there that this problem is getting worse?
3 What ailments do hedgehogs have that are not due to the climate?

1 What is the purpose of this text?
2 Why do you think the writer has put inverted commas around the word 'interfering'? (line 29)
3 What do you think 'poddle' means? (line 47)

1 How does the article make you feel about hedgehogs?
2 Does the article contain mostly facts, opinions or both? Use evidence from the text to support your answer.

Stretch zone

When you finish reading the article, go back and review words you didn't understand with a partner. Take turns to test each other on their meaning by looking at each of the words in its context in the sentence. Then look the words up in the dictionary and record the meanings.

What makes an effective newspaper article?

Almost all scientists believe that the way human beings live is having an effect on the Earth's climate. Many different consequences have been suggested, including the loss of some species of animals and plants, and changes in weather patterns.

You are going to prepare to write your own newspaper article alerting your readers to the dangers of climate change for wildlife. Read the fact file about polar bears on page 25. You will be using the information to create a news story of your own. Just like the writer of the article on hedgehogs on page 23, you will need to answer the questions the reader of your news article might have:

- What is the problem?
- What has caused the problem?
- What evidence is there?
- What can people do to help?

In small groups, discuss what else a reader might want to know and what features you need to include in a newspaper article. Make a checklist to help you to proofread and check your own article once you have written it.

Learning tip

Remember the difference between fact and opinion.

A **fact** is something which is backed up by evidence and can be checked.

For example: 'The Arctic is experiencing the warmest air temperatures for four centuries.'

An **opinion** is something which is based on a belief or view.

For example: 'Polar bears are the most magnificent creatures of the Arctic.'

Both facts and opinions can appear in a newspaper article.

- Read a range of texts and express opinions
- Read a non-fiction text and discuss its features

FACT FILE

- The Arctic's climate is changing and it is affecting polar bears.

- The Arctic is experiencing the warmest air temperatures for four centuries.

- In September 1979, when data collection began, there were 2.7 million square miles of sea ice in the Arctic.

  By September 2021, there were 1.8 million square miles — about two-thirds of what covered the Arctic in 1979.

- The Polar Bears International website (www.polarbearsinternational.org) states that there are 26,000 polar bears worldwide. Of these, 60% are in Canada.

- Polar bears are also found in the U.S. (Alaska), Russia, Greenland, and Norway.

- The website explains that the melting ice reduces the areas in which polar bears can hunt for food.

- In addition to climate change, other challenges to polar bears include increased commercial activities, conflicts with people, pollution, disease and inadequate habitat protection.

Tourists photograph a curious polar bear in Churchill, Canada

- Write a non-fiction newspaper article
- Write an organized text for a particular purpose
- Use a model text to help with own writing

Check your knowledge!

Make sure you understand the significance of the information in the fact file on page 25. This will help you with writing your newspaper article.

With a partner, read the fact file then test each other on the information in it by asking each other these questions:

- What is happening to sea ice in the Arctic?
- How does this affect the polar bears?
- How many polar bears are there in Canada?
- Apart from climate change, what other factors are affecting polar bears?

Do further research to find out more about polar bears and the risks they are facing. Identify places on the map below where polar bears roam.

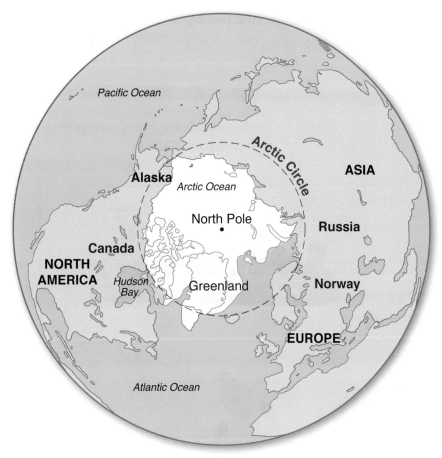

Map of the Arctic, showing the North Pole

Learning tip
Writing important information down as bullet points is a great way to help remember it while you conduct your research.

Language tip
Persuasive writing techniques will encourage your readers to take action. For example, you could include statistics, use repetition, directly address the reader, and use emotive, expressive language.

Tell the readers about your findings

Utilize the answers to the questions above, the notes about newspaper article features you made in the activity on page 24, and the rest of the fact file to write your own newspaper article about how polar bears are affected by climate change. Remember to use the article about hedgehogs on page 23 as a model for your own writing, and begin with an eye-catching phrase or question to grab the reader's attention.

* Read a range of texts and express opinions

How is climate change affecting the way people live?

Look back at the map on page 11 showing Bangladesh and its river delta. Why do you think the country suffers from frequent floods? Bangladesh is one of the countries in the world most vulnerable to the effects of climate change. 80% of the land area is floodplain and 18% of it floods each year. Floods make life difficult for many of the 167 million inhabitants (as of December 2021), most of whom have little money. Glaciers in the Himalayas have melted more than in the past, and Bangladesh is losing farmland due to rivers eroding river banks. Twenty million people unable to farm their flooded land could become 'climate refugees'. One successful method of protecting houses from flooding has been to build them up on platforms so that they will be above any flood water.

Glossary

glacier huge mass of ice slowly moving over the land down towards rivers, lakes or the sea

the Himalayas large mountain range in Asia, to the north of Bangladesh

Language tip
Remember the difference between **affect** and **effect**.

Affect is usually a verb and means to change or impact.

Effect is usually a noun and means the result of a change.

Severe flooding hits the Bangladeshi capital of Dhaka

Glacier near Gorakshep in the Nepalese Himalayas

- Read non-fiction texts and discuss their features

Have you ever heard of a school boat?

Bangladesh is a country on a mission to grow and improve the lives of the people who live there. There are several projects planned for the future that will make sure that all children have access to schools and learning. Abdul is a 12-year-old boy who lives in an area of Bangladesh which floods regularly. Read his school composition below, and find out about his good news.

Glossary

kerosene type of fuel sometimes used for heating, also called paraffin

The Best Day of My Life

I'm so excited! It was the first day of term today. Last year we couldn't get to school on a great many days because of the floods. Sometimes it was weeks. By the time I got back to school, I'd forgotten everything. It was very frustrating
5 because I want to study to be an architect when I'm older. If I miss school all the time, I will never succeed. Our father told us the situation was getting worse. He would often complain, saying, "We have no electricity and no cars and yet we suffer these terrible cyclones and storms caused
10 by the rich people in other countries."

But on this day of my life, everything was different. The best day: the school boat was coming! From now on it was going to come every day except Sunday and stay for three hours. My little sister, Maki, and I were ready an hour before it was
15 due to arrive. I held her hand tightly as we waited with all the other children at the edge of the water. We were all fizzing like bottles of lemonade and Maki was jumping up and down. She had missed much more school than I had. Our parents had been afraid to let her walk to school even
20 when it was open because of the dangerous water.

Suddenly we could see the school boat gliding along the flood waters and we all cheered so loudly I'm sure they could have heard us in Dhaka! Although we all wanted to rush on board immediately, it docked, we lined up as we
25 were told, and walked on board respectfully. Oh, what a paradise met our eyes!

Language tip
'**If**' or **conditional clauses** tell you if something happens, then something else will happen as a result.
For example: 'If I miss school, I will not succeed.'

Learning tip
This school composition uses **paragraphs** to **structure** and **organize** the information being shared. This helps the reader to understand.

Abdul talks about his day **chronologically** (meaning in time order). He talks about the **past** in the first paragraph, the events of **today** in the middle paragraphs, and what he imagines for the **future** in the last paragraph.

- Read non-fiction texts and discuss their features

There were forty seats on the deck for us older children, and benches for twenty little ones in the bow. We had books and pens and there were even solar-powered computers and a library for students older
30 than us. The three hours passed so quickly that I could not believe it when it was time to go home again.

But the best was not yet over! We were each given a solar lamp to take home so we could do homework. Before, we could never do any school work at home because our kerosene lamp was expensive to
35 run, and it also polluted the air and made a nasty smell.

Now I really do believe I will be able to study and succeed and become an architect. Then I will design more boats for our people, not just school and library boats, but for living in and for floating gardens where we could grow crops.

Bangladeshi children on a school boat

- Explain how language features create effects
- Give own opinions clearly and confidently

Comprehension

1 Describe some of the problems Abdul had with his schooling before the school boat was introduced.

2 Why is the school boat particularly exciting for Maki?

3 Why do you think the three hours pass so quickly for Abdul?

4 What are the benefits of a 'solar lamp' for Abdul and his family?

1 Which word or phrase could you use that means the same as 'suffer' in paragraph 1?

2 Find the simile used by Abdul in paragraph 2. What does this tell you about his emotions?

3 Which adverb tells you about the way the children went on board the school boat? (paragraph 3)

4 What does 'solar-powered' mean? (line 29)

1 What are the main differences between your school and Abdul's?

2 Compare Abdul's views on school and education with your own. What are the similarities and differences? Copy the table below and fill it in with your ideas. Then share your ideas with your group.

Language tip

A **simile** is a comparison of two dissimilar things, using the words 'like' or 'as'.

For example:
'The snow lay <u>like</u> a blanket over the fields.'

'Her hair is <u>as</u> white <u>as</u> snow.'

A **metaphor** goes one step further for poetic effect to make a direct statement (without using 'like' or 'as'). Metaphors describe things as if they were something else.

For example:
'A <u>blanket of snow</u> lay over the field.'

'The forest is an <u>ocean of trees</u>.'

<u>Comparison between my school and Abdul's</u>

Similarities   Differences

A solar lamp

Read Abdul's composition on pages 28 and 29 again. How would the children's lives be affected if they weren't able to use the school boat?

- Give own views and
  question views of others

Future climate change

Different landscapes around the world could be affected by changes in climate. Study the pictures.

In small groups, suggest how each of these landscapes and its inhabitants could be affected if the temperature rose by a significant amount.

- Match the following landscape words with the picture you think each fits: *prairie, woodland, rainforest, desert, bush*
- Suggest countries where you might find each of these different kinds of landscape.

- Identify and discuss ideas in poems

Forest fires and climate change

One of the most devastating effects of long spells of hot, dry weather is the potential for fires to start and spread rapidly. There are various causes of bush fires and forest fires. Some scientists believe that climate change is causing fiercer and more deadly fires. In the poem below, Jackie Kay, who was brought up in Scotland, writes about a raging bush fire in Australia.

Bush Fire

That fire, they said, was red as red as red
as red as a fox, your lips, a cherry;
that fire, they said, spread and spread and spread,
faster than a cheetah or a nasty rumour;
5   that fire, they said, was hot, so hot, so hot,
hotter than lava or an African summer.

That fire, they said, was angry, very angry.
For three roaring days, it danced wildly, wildly, wildly.
Wild as flamenco, strip-the-willow, a Highland fling.
10   That fire, they said, had a big bad mouth,
swearing, spluttering, 'Bring it on! Bring it on!'

That fire, they said, wolfed down the lot –
the lovely little homes, the trees, the land.
That fire, they said, left nothing behind at all:
15   one blackened trail, one sad scorched story.

JACKIE KAY

Glossary

flamenco traditional Spanish dance
strip-the-willow; **Highland fling** traditional Scottish dances

Language tip
Personification is a literary device where a quality, idea or other non-human thing is represented as though it were human.

For example: 'The sun smiled down as we enjoyed our picnic.'

- Identify and discuss ideas in poems
- Explain how language features create effects

Traditional Highland fling dancing

Flamenco dancing

Comprehension

1 With what does the writer compare the fire to create similes? Choose three comparisons and explain why they give added meaning to the text.

2 Flamenco, strip-the-willow and the Highland fling are all very energetic dances. Why do you think these dances make appropriate comparisons for the raging fire?

3 What do you think the verb phrase 'wolfed down' means? (line 12)

4 How do the repeated 's' sounds add to the description of the fire?

5 How does the poem use personification to describe the fire?

6 Repetition is used throughout the poem. Find examples and explain the effect these have on the mood of the poem.

Can you picture a forest fire?

The following extract is by Peter Godwin, who was born and raised in Zimbabwe. Read his description of a forest fire and think about how his words help you create a picture in your mind.

- Use features in a poem as a model for own writing
- Use literary devices to make writing interesting
- Use knowledge of language and text structure when writing

A cavern of flame

It was already gigantic when we arrived, a cavern of flame that soared ten storeys into the sky and blotted out the stars. A wall of intense heat blew off it and it was impossible to get anywhere near. The noise, too, was tremendous. Above the background
5   roar, there were constant crashes as trees collapsed. Hundreds of birds wheeled about, calling in alarm at their destroyed nests and their lost young. And a barrage of wild animals came bowling out of the fire towards us, crazed by fear.

From *Mukiwa* by PETER GODWIN

Now it's your turn to be a poet

Write your own poem about the forest fire described above. You could use the poem on page 32 as a model.

- In small groups, make a list of all the words you have read about fire and its effects. Think of other words that describe how fire can be seen, heard and felt.
- Turn your words into vivid phrases. You could think of some metaphors of your own, like the fire's 'big bad mouth' in the poem on page 32, or the 'cavern of flame' in the description above.
- Read and give feedback on each other's ideas. Use some ideas from others in your group to improve your own.
- Use your phrases to write your own poem that describes the fire in the description above.

Learning tip
Use a thesaurus to give yourself a choice of suitable, interesting vocabulary for your writing.

Understanding weather forecasts

Do you ever listen to or read weather forecasts? Forecasting the weather is a complex and scientific process. The results that weather scientists gather also provide information on issues like climate change. Forecasts are still only predictions, but what is certain is that the weather is very different around the world at any one time. Read the following weather forecasts for two different cities (Adelaide in Australia and Aberdeen in Scotland) from 20 January 2022.

- Discuss weather forecasts seen on television
- Write an organized text for a particular purpose
- Present a weather forecast using suitable visual images
- Choose an appropriate register to write in

Sunny and very warm. Clear skies with no rain expected. Temperature today in Adelaide: 24°C to 33°C.

Sunny spells with potential cloud. Some chance of rain. Temperature today in Aberdeen: 3°C to 4°C.

Talk about ...
- Why are these weather forecasts for the same day so different?
- What is the weather usually like in your country in January?

Be a weather presenter

Write a weather forecast like the ones above for your local area. You could choose to write about today's weather or make it up for your favourite time of year.

Watch a weather forecast being presented on television. Write your weather forecast out as a script and prepare a weather map to go with it, just as it would be seen on television. Prepare to present your forecast in small groups in class.

 Stretch zone

Find out and be ready to explain the difference between 'weather' and 'climate'.

What might a weather presenter say?

Heavy showers are forecast in ...
Extreme heat is expected in ...
There will be possible floods in ...
There will be strong winds in ...
It will stay mostly cloudy in ...
Thunderstorms are forecast in ...
There are warnings of heavy snow in ...

3 Air

What does the air we breathe mean to you?

> **To one who has been long in city pent,**
> **'Tis very sweet to look into the fair**
> **And open face of heaven.**
>
> From 'To One Who Has Been Long in City Pent'
>
> by JOHN KEATS

Talk about ...

- What is the difference between mountain air and sea air? What is the air like in big cities?
- Discuss what the air is like where you live.
- What do you know about the effects of air pollution?

Think about what the air was like when you set off for school this morning. What could you smell?

In the quotation above, the nineteenth-century English poet, John Keats, describes the pleasure of being in the open air after spending a lot of time in the city of London.

This unit will explore what the air means to different people and how it affects their lives.

Glossary

pent poetic word for 'penned', meaning shut up in a pen or fenced enclosure

'tis poetic abbreviation for 'it is'

No one owns the air

The writer of the following poem, Nicolás Guillén, came from Cuba. He believed that the air we breathe belongs to no one. This means that we all share it and we should look after it. It is difficult to describe the feeling and movement of fresh air, but this poet has used words and images in an original way to try to capture its effects.

- Identify and discuss ideas in poems
- Explain how language features create effects
- Learn new vocabulary by reading a variety of poems

from Can You?

Can you sell me the air that slips through your fingers,
strokes your face and tangles your hair?
Perhaps you could sell me five dollars' worth of wind,
or more, perhaps sell me a storm?
5 Perhaps you could sell me the delicate air
(not all of it) that dances
in your garden, from flower to flower,
dances in your garden among the birds,
ten dollars' worth of pure air?
10   The air spins and flits away
      Like a butterfly.
      No one owns it, no one.

Can you sell me some sky,
the sky that's sometimes blue
15 and sometimes grey,
a small strip of your sky,
the piece you think you bought with all the trees
in your orchard, as one buys the roof along with the house?
Can you sell me a dollar's worth
20 of sky, two miles
of sky, a slice of your sky,
whatever piece you can?
      The sky is high in the clouds.
      The clouds float by.
25   No one owns them, no one.

NICOLÁS GUILLÉN

This poem has been translated from Spanish.

> ◉ **Stretch zone**
>
> Think about the meaning of the following words taken from the poem.
>
> - to tangle (line 2)
> - delicate (line 5)
> - among (line 8)
> - to flit (line 10)
>
> Check their meaning in a dictionary and then use them in sentences of your own.

Comprehension

1 How does the poet describe the sky?

2 What don't you get included when you buy a house?

1 How does it feel if the air 'slips through your fingers'? (line 1)

2 What is the poet trying to say by using the word 'dances'? (lines 6 and 8)

3 What is the effect of using the word 'perhaps' several times in the first stanza?

4 What do you think is suggested by the word 'flits'? (line 10)

5 How does the poet create a sense of what the air is like to touch and feel?

1 What other things can you think of that no one owns and that no one can buy?

- Identify and discuss ideas in poems
- Explain how language features create effects
- Use clues in a poem to answer questions
- Perform poems with expression
- Talk about the differences between written and spoken language

Glossary

stanza section of a poem consisting of two or more lines. Stanzas can be rhyming but this is not always required.

Have a go at performing

Poetry is often intended to be read aloud. You will be reading the extract from the poem 'Can You?' on page 37 as a class performance.

- On a copy of the poem, highlight each question the poet has used in a different colour.
- Highlight the two three-line answers and the title in another colour.
- In small groups, discuss how the questions and answers should be spoken. For example, what happens to the tone of your voice when you ask a question?
- Share your ideas with the rest of the class and decide on how you will perform the poem as a whole class.

How does hearing the poem read out loud help you understand it better?

Language tip
Writers often use the repetition of sounds for poetic effect. This is called **alliteration**. You can use words that begin with the same sound, but often use different letters, like 's', 'sh' or 'z', to make a hissing or whispering sound.

What is a breath of fresh air?

Think about being in the countryside and breathing in fresh air. What do the clouds look like? How could you paint a picture of the wind in the sky?

Before the invention of photography, English painters like John Constable tried to capture wind, light and weather.

- Use clues in the painting to answer questions
- Be adventurous with sentences and language to create an effect

Landscape with Grey Windy Sky, by John Constable, painted in 1821–30

Comprehension

1 What do you think the air would smell like in this painting?
2 What does the air smell like where you are now?

1 How successful do you think the artist has been in creating the effect of wind and the movement of the clouds?
2 Describe the weather in the painting using a range of adjectives, similes and metaphors.

1 How can spending time watching the sky make us feel? Why do you think so many artists are drawn to painting the sky?

Crossing the field

Write a description of what it would be like to be crossing the field shown in the painting.

- Describe the sights, sounds and smells.
- Make it sound real by starting out with a reason for why you might be there. Perhaps you are taking a shortcut on your way home.

- Read a variety of texts and consider their features
- Discuss the context and setting of a story

A story about fog in London

In the opening chapter of his famous novel *Bleak House*, the English writer Charles Dickens describes the thick fog that sometimes descended on London in the 1830s.

Fog

Smoke lowering down from chimney-pots, making a soft black drizzle with flakes of soot in it as big as full-grown snow flakes … Fog everywhere. Fog up the river … fog down the river … fog in the eyes and throats of old men wheezing by their firesides
5 … people peeping over the bridges into a sky of fog, with fog all round them, as if they were up in a balloon, and hanging in the misty clouds.

From *Bleak House* by CHARLES DICKENS

Talk about …

- How does this impression of London in the 1830s differ to how you picture London today?
- Why are there differences?

A painting of London in the fog

The London fog Dickens describes was thick and harmful because of the pollution from burning coal and wood in people's homes and workshops. Some artists, such as Claude Monet, liked to paint their interpretation of the fog's effects and its sometimes strange beauty. On the following page is a painting by Monet from 1904, showing the Houses of Parliament at Westminster in an interesting dark and colourful light.

Language tip
Dickens uses **noun phrases** made up of one or more words that accompany the noun. These may be a series of adjectives or a determiner (an article or another word that indicates quantity).

For example: 'a soft black drizzle'.

- Read a variety of texts and consider their features
- Use clues in a text and a painting to answer questions
- Contribute to discussions and add own ideas

Houses of Parliament, Effect of Sunlight in the Fog, by Claude Monet

Comprehension

A

1 In Dickens's London, where did the smoke go when it came out of the chimney pots?
2 What could the people on the bridges see?
3 What was the cause of the pollution in London in the 1830s?

B

1 Describe the painting *Houses of Parliament, Effect of Sunlight in the Fog* in your own words, using descriptive vocabulary.
2 What do you think of the blurry effect to show the fog?
3 How would you feel if you were in fog like this?

C

1 Find out why pollution in the air is a hazard.
2 Is all pollution visible?
3 How important do you think clean air is? Is it a human right?

We can only breathe the air which is available to us. Human beings are unable to survive more than several minutes without it. Long-term exposure to high levels of air pollution can cause or worsen dangerous health conditions, especially in vulnerable people like young children and the elderly. Whose responsibility is it to ensure we have clean, healthy air to breathe? Is it fair that many people around the world have so little control over the quality of the air they breathe?

A story about fog in Scotland

It was not just London which suffered these terrible fogs. Here the writer Bill Paterson remembers his childhood in the 1950s in Glasgow, Scotland. Until 1962, the city of Glasgow had trams that ran on metal tracks in the roads.

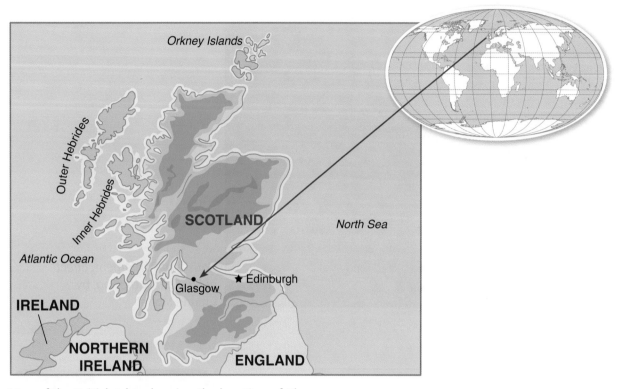

Map of the British Isles showing the location of Glasgow

Glasgow fog

And then there was the fog. It wasn't only London that had deep and dirty fogs in those days. Glasgow had some really thick ones when you couldn't see your hand in front of your face. I once walked into a lamp-post on my way to the school
5 swimming gala. When I got to the swimming baths an hour later they had cancelled it. It had not been cancelled for respiratory health reasons, but because you couldn't see one end of the indoor pool from the other.

When fog like that came down, the city trams were the only
10 vehicles which could move. They were the only things sure of where they were going. The city was already fixed beneath their wheels. Solid on their steel tracks, and lit from end to end, they crept along like ghostly ships. For most of the year,

Glossary

swimming gala special event where pupils compete against each other, or another school, in swimming

respiratory medical term that describes the function of breathing

murk gloomy darkness (the adjective 'murky' is more commonly used than the noun 'murk')

- Explain how language features create effects
- Compare fiction and non-fiction texts
- Understand the purpose of a text

15 the car, bus and lorry drivers thought the slow-moving trams were a nuisance. But when the smog came down, they followed the trams like ducklings following their mother.

"What number's that?" an unseen car driver would call out from the murk.

20 "It's an 8!" the conductor would call back.

The car driver would then follow the tram, knowing that he would make it into town. In the end the 25 smokeless zones cleared the fogs, and the buses and cars brought an end to the trams.

From *Tales from the Back Green* by BILL PATERSON

A tram moving through the foggy streets in 1950s Glasgow, Scotland

Comprehension

1 Why was the swimming gala cancelled?
2 Explain what the writer means when he says about the trams, 'The city was already fixed beneath their wheels'. (lines 11–12)
3 Usually car drivers found the trams a nuisance. Why did they change their minds when it was foggy?

1 Write down two similes from the text. Explain the comparison the writer makes in each one.
2 The word 'smog' is made up of two words joined together. Can you work out what the two words are?

1 In small groups, compare the fiction extract on page 40 with the autobiographical account 'Glasgow fog'. List differences and similarities between them.
2 Cities around the world, such as Jakarta (Indonesia), San Francisco (USA), Mexico City (Mexico), and Moscow (Russia), are often photographed blanketed in smog. Why is smog more dangerous to our health than fog and what can be done to reduce it?

Discovering history and culture in the open air

Have you heard of Angkor Wat in Cambodia? Maybe you have even been there. It is a magnificent ancient temple complex that was built in the first half of the twelfth century by Suryavarman II. It covers more than 400 acres (162 hectares)! In 1992, UNESCO declared Angkor Wat to be a World Heritage Site. Read the information below which introduces an audio tour of Angkor Wat and imagine you are there. Then read the article on the next page about Angkor and air pollution.

- Read a variety of texts and consider their features
- Summarize a text and understand its purpose

Glossary

causeway raised track across wet ground

Welcome to Angkor Wat

Welcome to one of the most significant archaeological sites in the world! Angkor Wat means 'Temple City'. The moat that surrounds Angkor Wat is 220 metres wide and 5.5 km in length. Access the enormous temple complex via the west entrance, walking along a causeway that is guarded by lions. This causeway takes you to a terrace that is in the shape of a plus sign. Continue walking and in the centre of the temple you will find five towers, the largest, central tower surrounded by four smaller ones. Be sure to find the carved wall friezes, including the *Churning of the Ocean of Milk*. After visiting Angkor Wat, you must go on to see other sites, such as the tree-root covered Ta Prohm Temple and the Bayon Temple complex.

- Read a variety of texts and consider their features
- Summarize a text and understand its purpose

Protecting Angkor

Angkor is one of the most important archaeological sites in the world but time, tourism, pollution and acid rain have taken their toll.

5 The ancient structures have been crumbling under the weight of in excess of 2.5 million tourists a year and increasing air pollution has resulted in acid rain that has caused decay and discolouration of the stone. This has caused great concern.

Old, carbon-dioxide emitting tourist buses have added to the air pollution, with vehicles running their engines while waiting
10 for tourists to board.

Water droplets in clouds contain pollutants that rain down, causing erosion of statues such as the carvings of the lions. Repair work has been carried out at Angkor Wat in recent years.

15 To lessen the effects of air pollution, the use of electric buggies and bikes at Angkor has been looked into. However, the cost of replacement batteries and a shortage of electricity are disadvantages that need to be addressed.

Glossary

archaeological relating to the study of history through digging up sites and remains

carbon dioxide poisonous gas formed by the burning of carbon, especially as car fuel

Repair work at Angkor Wat

45

- Summarize a text and understand its purpose
- Give own views and question others' views

Comprehension

1 What is the purpose of the causeway?
2 What feature at Angkor Wat should you definitely see?
3 What has been suggested as a way of reducing air pollution?

1 Which words in the audio guide introduction on page 44 encourage the listener to continue on the tour?
2 In the second text, on page 45, what effect does the use of the word 'crumbling' have to describe the condition of the temple?
3 What is the purpose of each of the texts about Angkor?

1 Explain how tourism has contributed to the decay of Angkor Wat.
2 Can you think of another example where tourism has damaged a special site in your own country, or one you have visited?

Talk about ...

Many popular tourist destinations are in poor condition and need protection from the wear and tear caused by tourists, but tourism also often funds the repair of these sites. Should tourism be banned from these places?

Time to put on your headphones

An audio tour is a recorded commentary about the things in a museum, or the history of a place of interest, such as Angkor Wat. Visitors can listen to the narration as they walk around. An audio tour gives information about the history of a place and other background details.

On the next page, there is an example of a map of an outdoor audio trail in Dartmoor, a national park in the south of England. It shows the location of sites of interest around Postbridge, which lies in the centre of Dartmoor and is the home to one of the finest bridges in the country. It is believed to date back to medieval times. Listeners can stop and select a number to listen to the recorded commentary.

Write an open-air audio tour

Think of a place you know really well. It might be your school, the local park, your neighbourhood, a historical landmark in your town, or a place of interest you often visit on holiday.

Imagine that a tourist wants to take a tour around your chosen place. What do you want them to notice and find out about? Note down the stops you want them to make and write a script for an audio tour.

- The script can include historical information, facts and figures, stories from your own personal experience, or all of these things!
- Look at the texts on Angkor Wat and the Postbridge audio tour map below for ideas.
- Read your audio tour script to the class and see if they can guess the place you have chosen.
- Make a map leaflet to accompany your tour, and include the places of interest marked with an audio tour icon.

- Look at the features of an audio guide
- Write a non-fiction audio tour for a particular audience
- Write an organized text for a particular purpose

Postbridge Audio Walk (6 miles, 10 km)

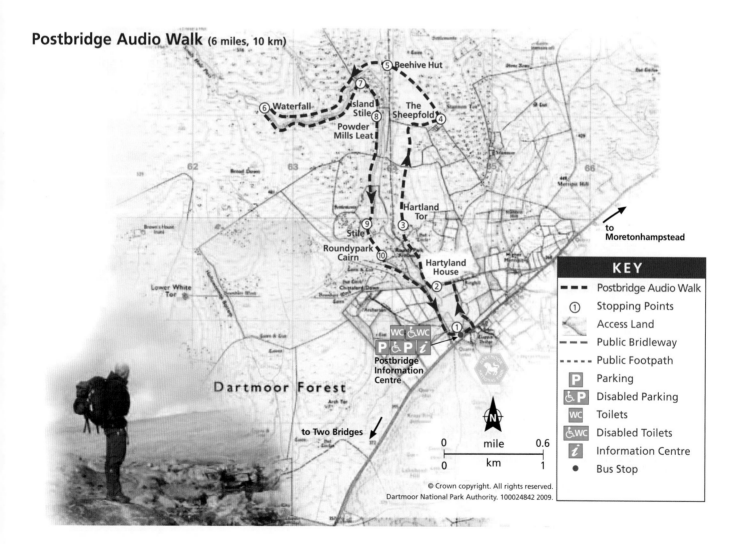

KEY

- - - - Postbridge Audio Walk
- ① Stopping Points
- ⟨ Access Land
- - - - Public Bridleway
- - - - - Public Footpath
- P Parking
- ♿P Disabled Parking
- WC Toilets
- ♿WC Disabled Toilets
- ℹ Information Centre
- ● Bus Stop

© Crown copyright. All rights reserved.
Dartmoor National Park Authority. 100024842 2009.

A story about a mysterious man – and mangoes

The following text is a mysterious story from Zanzibar. There is no pollution, but something quite different in the air!

Something in the Air

Suleiman was feeling happy, but a little anxious. He had just sold his last mango in the market. It was a good season this year and his fruit had sold well, but how long would this last? The sun was blazing down as usual as he counted his money,
5   zipped it inside his pouch and prepared to mount his bicycle for the journey home. Just as he took hold of the handlebars, he saw a man walking purposefully towards him. The man was wearing long, white Arab dress and a neat white cap.

"Asslaamu alaykum," the stranger said politely.

10   Suleiman barely had time to respond with "Wa alaykum salaam" before the man placed his hands on the handlebars and continued, "Suleiman, I have a job for you tomorrow, if you will do it."

Amazed that the stranger knew his name, Suleiman looked at him. Suddenly he felt a cool draught of air and noticed that
15   the man's light robe billowed on this hot, windless day.

"Don't be alarmed," the stranger continued. "I will pay you more for a day's work than you would earn in a year. I know you are the best mango picker in Zanzibar and I want you to harvest my mangoes. That is all. Will you meet me tomorrow
20   morning at Mnazi Mmoja at seven o'clock? I will take you to my mango orchard."

Suleiman stood dumbfounded and was just about to question the stranger when he disappeared into the bustle of the market. The cool draught had vanished along with the finely dressed
25   man. Suleiman stood motionless for a few minutes, dazed by what had happened.

Next morning, after a restless night, he wondered if he had dreamed it all.

"You may as well go to meet him," said his wife. "There are
30   no mangoes to sell today – you have nothing to lose."

Glossary

asslaamu alaykum Arabic greeting meaning 'Peace be upon you'. The traditional reply is *Wa alaykum salaam*, meaning 'And upon you be peace'.

draught current or stream of cool air

dumbfounded so surprised that you cannot speak

So Suleiman set off on his bicycle. It was an hour's ride to Mnazi Mmoja. When he arrived there was no mango orchard to be seen, but the stranger in white Arab dress was waiting for him. As Suleiman propped his bicycle against a tree, the
35 man approached him, and Suleiman again felt the cool draught. He shivered and saw the fine white robe billowing in the sudden wind. A moment later, the robe was perfectly still. The man smiled and greeted him politely, as before.

"Come with me and I will take you to my orchard, Suleiman,"
40 he said.

Suleiman greeted his employer and untied his baskets, which contained his ropes and large sharp knife, from his bicycle. After they had walked a few yards, Suleiman was about to ask where the mango orchard was when he was overwhelmed by
45 an intense perfume. Everything went black for a moment. When he opened his eyes again he found himself in the greenest and most beautiful orchard of mango trees he had ever seen.

"I will return at sunset," said the stranger with a smile, and suddenly he was gone.

- Explore how setting and character are developed

50 Suleiman started picking the fruit. They were wonderfully ripe. They smelled more sweetly and were more succulent than any mango he had seen in all his forty years. By sunset he had made a huge pile. There were more mangoes than he could possibly count.

55 At sunset the man returned. He was pleased with Suleiman's work and pressed his wages into his hand. It was just as he had promised: more money than Suleiman could hope to earn in a year. Suleiman picked up his baskets and ropes and was putting his knife away carefully in his pouch, with the money,
60 when he felt the cool draught. He looked up. The man had disappeared.

The intense perfume which had overwhelmed him in the morning suddenly enveloped him and again, everything was instantly black. When he opened his eyes, he was standing under the tree by his bicycle. There was no sign of the mango
65 orchard.

He tied his baskets onto his bicycle and started the long ride home. On his return his wife and little children gathered round him.

"Was he there? What happened?" asked his wife.

70 "I do not know," answered Suleiman and, feeling suddenly weak, he leaned against the table, and told his wife his tale.

When he finished the story, with trembling hands he took off his pouch, unsure whether the money, too, would prove to be some kind of dream. But there it was, and when his wife saw
75 it she danced around the house with the children.

Word origins

overwhelm (v), from the Old English *hwylfan*, meaning 'to upheave' or 'to submerge'
Related words:
- overwhelming
- underwhelm
- underwhelming

Comprehension

1 What surprises Suleiman about the stranger when he first approaches?

2 What is so special about the stranger's mango orchard?

3 What does Suleiman experience before and after he works in the stranger's orchard?

4 How does Suleiman feel when he returns to his home?

- Explore how setting and character are developed
- Use a model text to help with own writing
- Use knowledge of language and text structure when writing

B

1 What does the adverb 'purposefully' tell you about the way the stranger approaches Suleiman? (line 7)

2 Suggest an alternative to the word 'barely'. (line 10)

3 What does the word 'intense' tell you about the way the perfume smelled? (line 45)

4 Make a list of the words used to describe the stranger's mangoes.

5 Rewrite the sentence 'There was no sign of the mango orchard' using different words to say the same thing. (lines 64–65)

C

1 How would you describe the atmosphere that the writer creates in the story? Do you think it is typical of a mystery story?

2 Describe how and why Suleiman's feelings change through the story. How would you have felt in his position?

Write your own mystery story

Have you heard stories of strange, unexplained things happening? This is what mystery stories are often about. They are about something unusual that is not always fully explained and may contain strange coincidences.

- Write your own mystery story. You can make it up entirely. If you base it on a story you have heard in the past, try to give it an original twist of your own.
- Use the short story 'Something in the Air' as a model to guide you: include direct speech and descriptions of the strange experiences or events that occur.
- Alternatively, write a new ending to the story 'Something in the Air'. Use a mixture of ordinary words and very descriptive passages to emphasize the strange events.

Stretch zone

Find copies of mystery stories. Read the first couple of paragraphs and decide which hooks the reader the most and why.

Language tip
Comparative adjectives and adverbs are used to compare things. They are shown by an added *-er* at the end of an adjective, or using the word 'more' in front of an adjective or an adverb.

For example:
'sweeter', 'more succulent', 'more sweetly'.

Superlatives are used to describe the most extreme version of something, by adding *-est* at the end of an adjective, or putting the word 'most' in front of an adjective or adverb.

For example: 'the greenest and most beautiful orchard'.

4 Changing places

What happens when you move to another part of the world?

6 Give me your tired, your poor, Your huddled masses yearning to breathe free. 9

From the poem 'The New Colossus' by EMMA LAZARUS, on a plaque inside the pedestal of the Statue of Liberty in New York Harbor, USA

Talk about ...
- What do you think this quotation means?
- Why is it significant that it is on the Statue of Liberty?

People have moved from one country to another for thousands of years, sometimes from choice or often out of necessity. The reasons can be economic, often to find work, or social and driven by the desire to find a better quality of life. Some people move for political reasons, such as to escape war, and others move due to famine in their home country. Have you ever had to leave your home? If not, what do you think it must feel like?

- Choose an appropriate register to write in
- Write organized, structured texts

The Statue of Liberty

The 'Statue of Liberty Enlightening the World' was erected on Ellis Island in New York Harbor in 1886. It was a gift of friendship from the French people to commemorate the part they played in the American Revolution and the Declaration of Independence. It has stood ever since as a 'universal symbol of freedom and democracy'. It has traditionally been seen as a symbol of hope to all immigrants who come to New York to start a new life in America. Migration to the United States began all the way back in the sixteenth century.

Talk about ...
- Have you always lived in the country you are in now?
- Has anyone in your circle of family and friends moved to another country to start a new life? If so, share your experiences.

Familes from Europe arriving for a new life on *The Imperator* ocean liner in New York in 1913

Glossary

emigration moving from your country to live in another

immigration moving to another country that is not your own to live or work

migration animals or people travelling to a new place in large numbers

migrate move from one place to another

Writing a welcome message

Write a short message welcoming someone new to your country. What pieces of important information do you want to tell them? Discuss in a group whether it should be formal or informal.

- Understand the purpose of a text

A new life in America

All new immigrants to America in the first half of the twentieth century had to go to the Ellis Island immigration station, a short ferry ride from Liberty Island and New York City. From 1892 to 1954, 17 million people passed through Ellis Island.

How do you think the immigrants felt as they arrived on Ellis Island for processing?

5 The year 1907, when this photo was taken, was the peak year for immigration at Ellis Island, with 1,004,756 people processed. Generally, those immigrants who were approved spent from two to five hours on the island. People with obvious
10 health problems were held in the island's hospital facilities for a period of time. They all had to answer 29 questions, including their name, age, occupation (job), and how much money they had on them. Some immigrants were rejected
15 outright and sent back to where they came from.

It has been estimated that nearly half of all American citizens today can trace their family history to at least one person who passed through the Port of New York at Ellis Island.

An Italian immigrant family at Ellis Island, New York, waiting to be processed after their long sea voyage

Comprehension

1 Why do you think the people who had obvious health problems had to stay in the island's hospital?

2 What is the purpose of this text?

1 What does 'the peak year for immigration' mean? (line 6)

1 Discuss and make a list of some of the other questions you think the immigrants had to answer.

Ellis Island, with Liberty Island in the background

Life in pictures

People (and wildlife) have a wide variety of reasons for wanting to move from one place to another. Look carefully at what is happening in these pictures.

Talk about ...

Describe what is happening in each of these pictures.

"I can't earn enough money here to feed my family."

"We're starting a new life here in America."

"Look at the snow geese in perfect 'V' formation. They have flown a long way to get here from the Arctic."

"Should we ask Shareen if she wants to join us? It feels a bit awkward."

55

A story about emigration

Many people are forced to leave their home because of violence or war. The following story is about Shauzia, a 12-year-old girl who left Afghanistan after conflict made her country unsafe. She travelled across the border to a refugee camp in Pakistan, but she hated life in the camp. She dreamed of travelling to France and starting a new life. With her dog Jasper for company, Shauzia left the camp to follow her dream. She reaches the city of Peshawar, where she looks for work.

- Read a wide range of stories
- Consider how different grammatical features create meaning and organize ideas

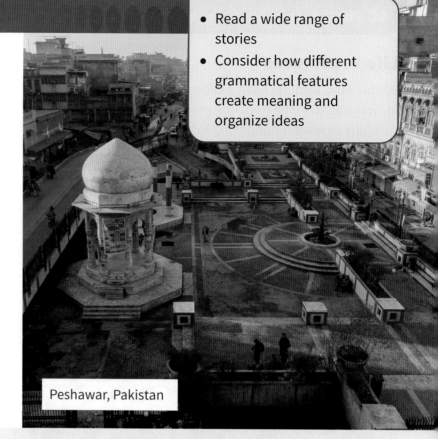

Peshawar, Pakistan

Shauzia's dream

Shauzia tried hard to find a job. She did many different ones, some lasting a few days, some just a few hours. In the cloth market, with rainbows of fabrics hanging over the walkway like a multicoloured forest, she helped unload the heavy bolts
5   of cloth, and put buttons into jars.

She cleaned the butcher's shop, and one day she set up sheep's heads on the table outside. The butcher gave her a good-sized bone for Jasper at the end of that day. He also recommended her to his friend who had a grocer's shop, and she got a day's
10   work there, cleaning the floor.

She got a few days' work delivering cups of tea while the tea shop's regular delivery boy was sick. She delivered trays of tea to merchants who couldn't leave their shops for a break. She was good at it, too, and could hurry through the narrow streets
15   of the market without spilling a drop. Everywhere she delivered tea, she asked if there was work for her. She was rewarded with a job sweeping out a furniture warehouse.

One day, instead of looking for work, she went to the train station. "Do any of these trains go to the sea?" she asked the
20   man behind the ticket counter.

> **Language tip**
> **Relative clauses** are subordinate clauses that modify a noun, often using 'who', 'where', 'what' or 'which'. They give extra information about the noun.
>
> For example: 'She delivered trays of tea to merchants <u>who couldn't leave their shops for a break</u>.'

- Use clues in a story to answer questions
- Write grammatically correct sentences

The ticket seller told her the price of a single ticket to the port city of Karachi. It was much, much more than she had saved. She turned away sadly and was almost back on the street when a man gave her a tip of a few rupees to carry his bundle to the train.

25

After that, on the days when she didn't have other jobs, she went to the train station and carried people's bags for tips. She couldn't go there often because the regular porters who were officially employed chased her away if they saw her.

30

It was just as well. She found it hard watching other people get on the trains when she longed to do so herself. When would it be her turn?

Each night she added more rupees to the soft purse hung around her neck. Each night she felt she was a little closer to the sea.

35

From *Mud City* by DEBORAH ELLIS

Comprehension

A

1 Why does Shauzia hang her purse around her neck?
2 What does Shauzia receive in return for carrying people's bags?
3 What does the final sentence tell you about how Shauzia felt and what she was dreaming of? (lines 36–37)

B

1 Look at the words with apostrophes. Explain why apostrophes are used in the following words, and why they are placed where they are:

a butcher's (line 6)   c people's (line 29)

b day's (line 9)   d couldn't (line 29)

C

Write a short paragraph on each of the following:

1 Which of Shauzia's jobs would you least like to do?
2 Do you think that Shauzia's dream of going to Europe will come true?

Language tip
Apostrophes can be used in two different ways: to show where letters have been missed out ('have not' / 'haven't') or to show ownership ('the cat's tail'). Find out what the rule for plural ownership is.

Learning the language

Learning a new language is a challenging task. So is keeping up with the language of the culture you were born into.

Mohammed Obadi is now 80. He left Yemen as a young man and has lived in Sheffield in the United Kingdom ever since. In the extract below, he looks back on his long life. When he first came to the UK, he did not learn 'proper' English and picked up what he could. Now he is taking special classes to learn the language systematically.

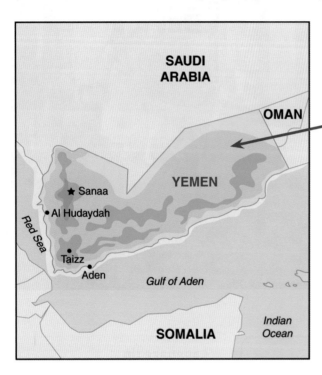

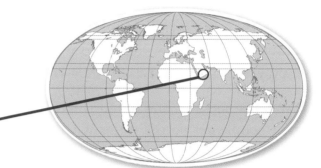

Learning English at last

Back in the late 1950s, there were no opportunities for young men in the Yemen. When we heard about jobs in the steelworks in Britain, we thought, "That's
5 what we'll do!" Thousands and thousands of us came over to Britain from Yemen to work in the steelworks. Sheffield was a big steel-producing city then.

I liked it here. I liked the hills round about
10 which reminded me of home, and I liked the city. The work was hard. Sometimes our shifts were sixteen hours but we didn't mind that. I worked as a 'spare man'. That

Men and boys in the 1950s in the port city of Aden, now part of Yemen

meant that I was skilled at every job so I could fill in for
15 anyone who was sick. I was highly skilled.

The conditions in the factories weren't good then. On one
occasion I went to the boss and I said, "Sir, the conditions
are not good. We Yemenis can't understand what the gaffer
says. We can't read the safety rules. We're often injured. We
20 want to have English lessons." Do you know what his
answer was? "English lessons! You're here to work, not
learn! Work, work that's what you're here for." That's what
it was like back then. So we'd work our long shifts and then
go to the Yemeni cafes and speak Arabic. Then, when the
25 steel industry collapsed, thousands of us were made
redundant. It was a terrible time.

But it's all different now. We've got the Yemeni Centre.
Yemenis who were born here in Britain learn Arabic so they
don't forget their roots. And what about me? I'm learning
30 English at last! I go to College once a week in a class of
retired Yemeni steelworkers who are all learning to speak
proper English. Our average age is 75! When we started we
only knew commands because that's all we'd ever heard. But
we're progressing really well now. We worked hard in the
35 steelworks, and now we're working hard with our English.
My friend is 81 and last year he won a special Learners'
Award!

Isn't life a funny thing? When I look back to when I was a
boy in my village in Yemen, it's like looking at another
40 person. Was that really me?

- Learn new vocabulary by reading different stories
- Work out the meaning of words by looking at the context
- Write questions that are suitable for an interview

Glossary

gaffer (*informal*) man in charge of other workers

Stretch zone

Look at these words, in the context of the text, and write down a definition for each.

- steelworks (line 7)
- shifts (line 12)
- to be skilled (line 14)
- conditions (line 16)
- to collapse (line 25)
- to be made redundant (lines 25–26)
- commands (line 33)

Writing interview questions

What would you like to ask Mr Obadi? Perhaps you would like to know more about his early life in Yemen, or what it was like when he first arrived in the UK. Does he feel nostalgic and sentimental about the country he used to live in?

Write some interview questions to ask him if you had the chance to meet him.

Yemeni men attending an English class in Sheffield

Life on the wing

It is not just people who move from one country to another. Many birds migrate between continents. Migration is a hazardous time for the birds. Many die of starvation and exhaustion, or in storms.

Stretch zone

Find out why birds migrate long distances every year. Write a short paragraph summarizing your findings.

Swallows gathered on telegraph wires in the UK, preparing to migrate

A hobby falcon is a bird of prey and an enemy to migrating swallows

A story about migrating birds

In this story, the swallows return each year to nest in a family's garage in England. A brother and a sister, Matt and Olly, watch them each year as they nest, lay their eggs and raise their young. But this year, Olly is alone because Matt is in Africa. When one of the baby swallows is injured by a neighbour's cat, Olly and her mother nurse it back to health. It is then able to join the other swallows on their migration at the end of the summer. Olly calls the swallow Hero, and hopes that it will find her brother in Africa. This part of the story describes the beginning of Hero's long and hazardous journey.

Barn swallow

Hero's journey

Hero joined the others as they flocked to a nearby lake, and for several days he hunted there, skimming over the water after mosquitoes. He was safe here with his family, amongst thousands upon thousands of gathering swallows and martins. All the
5 while, his strength grew within him. At dusk as darkness began to fall, they gathered to roost in the trees around the lake. Every night in the roost the air of expectancy grew. Every night the birds were slower to settle to their sleep.

Then one morning early, the hobby falcon came gliding high
10 over the lake. The birds heard his killer kew-kew call and scattered in terror.
Down came
the hobby falcon,
swifter than any bird Hero
15 had ever seen.
Hero felt the wind of
him as he passed by,
and swerved aside only
just in time. But the hobby falcon
20 was not after him, he was
after a young martin, slower
and more stuttering in flight than
Hero – and for the martin there
was no escape.

25 The flock flew that same morning. A whispering cloud of birds swirled out over the lake; the sky darkened as it went. They flew south towards the sea, hoping that they had seen the last of the hobby falcon. But the hobby falcon was not far behind, for he too was bound for Africa. He would fly all the way with
30 them, taking the youngest, the slowest, the weakest, whenever he felt like it. He had done it before.

From *Dear Olly* by MICHAEL MORPURGO

- Read a range of texts and express opinions
- Consider how different grammatical features create meaning and organize ideas

Comprehension

1 What happens to the birds that don't make it all the way to Africa?

2 Why is the hobby falcon so frightening to the migrating birds? How does the line spacing add to the effect?

1 Explain what kind of movements and activities are described in the following verbs: 'to flock'; 'to skim'; 'to gather'; 'to roost'; 'to settle'.

2 The movements of the hobby falcon are different from those of the swallows. Which words help you to imagine the hobby falcon's movements?

3 In the final paragraph, there are so many birds that they look like a cloud. Why do you think the author describes the cloud as 'whispering'? What caused the sky to darken?

1 What other animals can you think of that make long and dangerous journeys?

- Identify and discuss ideas in poems
- Give own opinions clearly and confidently

A poem about emigration

The noun 'alien' is a word sometimes used for a person from a very different family, people, or place. It is also used to mean a creature from outer space.

The writer of this poem uses the idea of an alien from outer space to describe how she felt as a schoolgirl when she first moved to England.

Alien Abduction

Snatched away on a not quite round silver saucer
To a world unknown, far away and alien
To me.

Abducted from my world.
5 What for?
'For your own good, for education, for ...'
They said.

They called this world England:
Small, contained, powerful
10 And surrounded by sea.

A solitary world inside a world –
Like me.

One of my kind –
Or so I felt.
15 Searching eyes and hostile glances
Scoured me each and every day,
Questioning my right to be here.

I was different:
A black-haired, brown-eyed
20 Blot in a white sea.

It took time for me to understand
That, alien as this country was to me,
An alien is what I was to them.
Would I ever be anything else?

Mariya Aziz

Comprehension

 A

1 Why do you think the writer has called the poem 'Alien Abduction'?

2 Who do you think 'they' refers to in line 7?

3 Why does the writer call England 'a solitary world inside a world'? (line 11)

 B

1 Why does the writer think of herself as 'alien'?

2 Why is an ellipsis used in line 6?

 C

1 Do you think the writer ever became happy after emigrating to England?

Read a letter

Do you ever write letters? Do you think writing a letter is different to writing an email? Why? Why not?

Here is a letter which a grandmother in Bogotá, Colombia wrote to her granddaughter who had emigrated to the UK with her parents.

> Cra. 146a - 3 Apto 702
> Edificio Real Bogotá
> Colombia
>
> 15 October
>
> Dear Luisa,
>
> You have been in England for six months now and I miss you more each day. I hope that you have settled into your new school now and that you are enjoying it. You must work hard and take advantage of the opportunities in your new country and make your parents proud of you.
>
> Please write and tell me all about your new life. Have you made some new friends? What is the city of Bath like? The buildings must be very different. I cannot imagine them. I am busy, but I am always thinking about my dear family so far away. Hopefully writing letters will give us both a chance to practise our English!
>
> Look after your mother and father and little sisters for me. I long to give you a big hug.
>
> With lots of love from
> Mamá Valeria

Learning tip

Letters often follow a set of conventions. In your letter to your grandmother, write three paragraphs and include:

- your postal address
- the date
- a salutation or greeting (such as 'Dear Granny', or whichever name you use)
- a sign-off phrase (such as 'love from' or 'with lots of love')
- your name (make up an appropriate one).

Read a wide range of stories
- Write a letter with accurate grammar, punctuation and a variety of sentence types
- Make sure text structure is suitable for its purpose

Now write a reply!

Imagine that you are a young person who has emigrated to another country, and you are writing a reply to a letter from your grandmother, or from another relative.

- Contribute to discussions and share own ideas
- Give own opinions clearly and confidently
- Use clues in a text and an image to answer questions

A new life in Australia

What do you know about the history of emigration to Australia? The population of Australia is made up of people from more than 200 countries.

According to the Australian government, 7.5 million migrants have arrived in the country since 1945. A large proportion of these immigrants arrived in the immediate post-war period. The Second World War (1939–45) had left many Europeans displaced and homeless.

Many people also left Europe voluntarily to start a new life. Between 1945 and 1972, Australia ran the Assisted Passage Scheme to encourage people from the United Kingdom to emigrate. British people paid only ten pounds for their fare, but had to stay for at least two years. Most travelled by boat, but some paid the difference to travel by air rather than sea. The photograph below is of families waving goodbye at London Airport in 1948.

Glossary

displaced forced to leave your country because of war; also known as being a 'refugee'

Judging by the photograph below, what sort of people were going to live in Australia in 1948?

- Design and make a poster that has a message
- Prepare notes to give a presentation

What is the message of this poster?

The picture below is a poster designed in 1948 to encourage people in the United Kingdom to emigrate to Australia.

Talk about ...

- What do you think people looking at the poster would imagine Australia was like?
- What do you think 'land of tomorrow' means?
- How successful do you think this poster was? Do you think it painted an accurate picture of life in Australia?

Design a poster

Keep in mind the things you noticed about the Australian poster shown above. Use the ideas from your discussion to help you create a successful design for a poster of your own.

- Make a poster to encourage new emigrants to come to any country you choose.

- Carry out research and prepare a talk to go with your poster to prepare people to go and live in the country you have chosen.

- Think of a slogan (a vivid phrase or sentence that promotes a message, such as 'land of tomorrow') for your poster.

- Discuss the context and setting of a story
- Work out the meaning of words by looking at the context
- Compare written and spoken English

Read an autobiographical essay

In the following extract, Amy Choi remembers her grandfather. Amy emigrated with her family, including her grandfather, from China to Australia as a child. When Amy was 16, her grandfather died.

Grandfather's language

I was never particularly kind to my grandfather. He was my mother's father, and he lived with us when I was a teenager. I remember him coming into the sitting room one night, and when he went to sit down, I said to my brother, "I hope he
5 doesn't sit down." I didn't think my grandfather understood much English, but he understood enough, and as I watched, he straightened up again, and without a word, returned to his room. I was twelve years old.

My grandfather wrote poetry on great rolls of thin white paper
10 with a paintbrush. He offered to read and explain his poems to me several times over the years, but I only let him do it once. I'd let my Chinese go by then, which made listening to him too much of an effort. Though I was raised speaking Chinese, it wasn't long before I lost my language skills. I spoke English
15 all day at school, listened to English all night on TV. I didn't see the point of speaking Chinese. We lived in Australia.

From Monday to Friday, Grandad went to the city, dressed in a suit with a waistcoat, a hat, and carrying
20 his walking stick. He would take the bus to the station, the train to the city, then the tram to Little Bourke Street. On Mondays, he'd be sitting at a large round table at
25 Dragon Boat Restaurant with other old Chinese men. Tuesdays to Fridays, he was at a small square table by himself with a pot of tea and the Chinese newspaper. I watched him
30 leave in the morning and come back

Talk about ...

The author uses some expressions commonly used in speech, but not in formal written English. Discuss what each of these expressions means:

- 'I'd let my Chinese go'
- 'Could barely string a sentence together'
- 'Whenever I am stuck for a word'
- 'Throw into a conversation'

in the afternoon, as punctual and as purposeful as any school child or office worker, for years.

At the funeral, my sadness was overshadowed by a sense of regret. I'd denied my grandfather the commonest of kindnesses.
35   I was sixteen years old. I am now twenty-six. A few weeks ago, during a family dinner at a Chinese restaurant, the waiter complimented my mother on the fact that I was speaking to her in Chinese. The waiter told Mum with a sigh that his own children could barely string a sentence together in Chinese.
40   Mum told the waiter I had stopped speaking Chinese a few years into primary school, but that I had suddenly started up again in my late teens.

I have often wondered how aware my mum is of the connection between Grandad's death and my improving Chinese. Whenever
45   I am stuck for a word, I ask her. Whenever I am with her, or relatives, or a waiter at a Chinese restaurant, or a sales assistant at a Chinese department store, I practise. I am constantly adding new words to my Chinese vocabulary, and memorising phrases I can throw into a conversation. It is my way of re-learning a
50   language. Textbooks and teachers are not necessary, since I am only interested in mastering the spoken word. I am not trying to 'discover my roots'. I am simply trying to ensure that the next time an elderly relative wants me to listen, I am not only willing, I am able.

From *The Relative Advantages of Learning My Language* by AMY CHOI

- Write an autobiographical story
- Plan your story, proofread it and correct errors
- Write grammatically correct sentences
- Be adventurous with sentences and language to create an effect
- Vary the sentences you write by including different types of conjunctions

Ink, brushes and paper for writing in Chinese

Writing an autobiography

Think about a memorable event that has happened in your life and write a story about it. Include details about:

- Setting: when and where did it happen?
- Characters: who else is involved?
- Events: what happened to make the event interesting and memorable?
- Reflections: did this experience change you and/or the way you look at the world and yourself?

Make sure you include plenty of description so that the reader feels like they are involved in the story.

How do humans respond to and understand natural disasters?

> *Forests were set on fire ...*
> *and the crackling trunks*
> *Extinguished with a crash –*
> *and all was black.*
>
> From 'Darkness' by LORD BYRON

Talk about ...

- How would you feel if there was complete darkness, day and night?
- What would it be like if you were not able to see the sun, the moon or the stars? How would you feel?

Word origins

catastrophe (n), from the ancient Greek word *katastrophe,* meaning 'a sudden turning' (*kata* means 'downwards'). Today, we use the word for natural disasters caused by earthquakes, tidal waves, forest fires, and volcanoes.
Related words:
- catastrophic
- cataclysmic

Tens of thousands of people are killed every year by catastrophic events: earthquakes, volcanic eruptions, tsunamis, floods, droughts, wildfires, hurricanes and pandemics. They are usually sudden, natural events that cause destruction and death, as it is not always possible for people to prepare adequately.

The dark summer of 1816

In 1815, the volcano Mount Tambora erupted in Indonesia. About 80,000 people on two Indonesian islands were killed. The results of the eruption were catastrophic for people around the world.

As a result of the 1815 Tambora volcano eruption, dust was released into the Earth's atmosphere, blotting out the sun. Temperatures were reduced across the whole planet. It was a year of very poor harvests and a shortage of food because crops could not grow. Because of this, 1816 was known in Europe as the 'year without a summer'.

It was this dark summer of 1816 that the English poet Lord Byron described in the quotation on page 68, taken from his poem 'Darkness'. Here are some more lines from the same poem.

- Discuss the context and setting of a poem
- Explain how language features create effects
- Work out the meaning of words by looking at the context

Glossary

darkling poetic way of saying 'in the dark'

rayless rays of light from the stars no longer seen on Earth

Darkness

I had a dream, which was not all a dream.

The bright sun was extinguished, and the stars

Did wander darkling in the eternal space,

Rayless, and pathless, and the icy Earth

5   Swung blind and blackening in the moonless air;

Morn came and went – and came, and brought no day.

Comprehension

1 Describe what is happening in the poem.

1 Lord Byron uses a lot of imagery in the extract from 'Darkness'. Find one example and explain it as fully as possible in your own words.

1 Look back to the explanation of the dark summer of 1816 at the top of the page. Discuss the differences between this account of the catastrophe and that in Lord Byron's poem.

 Stretch zone

Think about the meaning of the following words taken from the quotation on page 68 and the poem above:

- to crackle
- trunk
- to extinguish
- eternal

Make your own list of any other unfamiliar words you come across. Look the words up in a dictionary and record the meanings.

- Read a non-fiction text and discuss its features

What is a volcano?

What do you know about volcanoes? The extract below from the *How Stuff Works* website gives some introductory information about volcanoes.

How volcanoes work

Every so often you hear about a major volcanic eruption somewhere in the world. Of course, there are many news stories that cover the event or catastrophe. People throughout history have been in awe of the sight or description of a raging, violent volcano. How can a quiet, peaceful mountain suddenly become a terrifying and transforming force?

So what is a volcano? Under the Earth's crust or surface is the mantle which is made up of extremely hot rock. When the Earth's plates move away or towards each other, it can cause the mantle to melt and move around. Sometimes the melted mantle or magma fills in gaps under the Earth's crust. If there is no room, the magma can be forced out of the Earth's crust to form a volcano. Sometimes a volcano can happen under the ocean. Sometimes the magma will spread out along the bottom of the ocean and magma is spewed out above the surface of the water.

www.howstuffworks.com

Glossary

magma hot liquid rock found underground

Earth's plates huge sections of the Earth's crust that move around; the plates are from 50 to 250 miles thick

Word origins

volcano (n), from the Latin *Volcanus*, meaning 'Vulcan', the Roman ruler of fire
Related word:
- volcanic

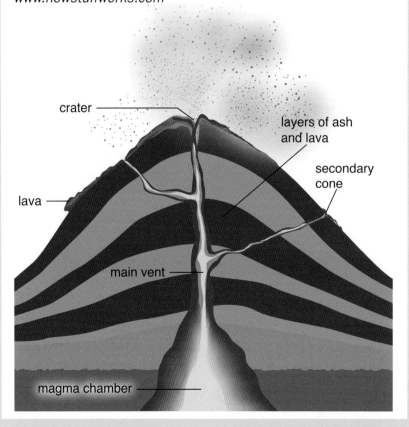

The eruption of Mount Vesuvius, 79 CE

Mount Vesuvius is situated in the Bay of Naples in Italy. It is one of the most active volcanoes in the world, yet 3,000,000 people live close to it. Its most recent eruption was in 1944. Its most famous and catastrophic eruption, in 79 CE, resulted in the destruction of the Roman cities of Pompeii and Herculaneum. The remains of these cities are visited by thousands of people every year.

There is a vivid description of the eruption in the letter of a Roman known as Pliny the Younger. In these letters, he describes his uncle, Pliny the Elder, trying to save people on the other side of the Bay of Naples, close to the eruption. The text on the next page is part of a description of the events of that night. Pliny's description of the eruption was so detailed that scientists who study volcanoes named a type of eruption, the 'Plinian', after him.

Rewrite a text

A text written by Pliny the Younger is over the page, but you must not look at it until you have completed this task! First, your teacher will read the text to you.

- As your teacher reads the text for the first time, listen carefully.
- While your teacher reads it for the second time, you may take some brief notes.
- With a partner, rewrite what you remember of the text informally in your own words.

- Write grammatically correct sentences with correct punctuation
- Summarize a text

Talk about ...

- Look at the diagram of the inside of a volcano on page 70 and take turns to explain to each other the parts of the volcano.
- How useful is the diagram in helping you to understand how volcanoes work?
- What does it mean to be 'in awe' of the destructive power of nature?
- Name some volcanoes from different countries. Carry out some research if you can't think of any.

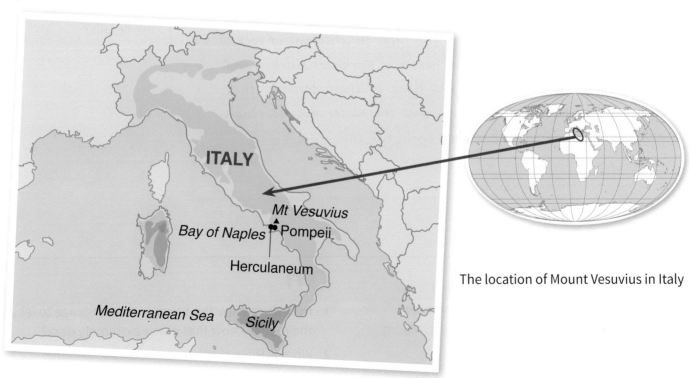

The location of Mount Vesuvius in Italy

- Read a wide range of texts
- Use clues in a text to answer questions

Read an eye-witness account

Pliny the Younger's letter describes his observation of the eruption of Mount Vesuvius and his uncle's efforts to save people's lives.

My uncle Pliny ordered ships to be made ready and they set out across the bay. He was anxious to save as many of the people living at the foot of Vesuvius as he could. It was a great adventure to him as he was a keen scientist and he could observe the changing shapes
5 and colours of the great cloud. Ash was now falling onto the ships.

As they drew closer to land, the atmosphere became darker and denser. Pieces of rock burned and blackened by the fire landed on the ships' decks. The sea was so thick with debris that they could not approach the land. So they sailed to the other side of the bay
10 and into the harbour. Ships there were ready to evacuate the inhabitants, but were trapped by the wind, unable to escape. Broad sheets of brilliant flame were now lighting up many parts of the mountain as my uncle and his men hurried into a nearby house. Its floors rose and fell as ash and stone flowed beneath them. Then
15 it was rocked by strong tremors and began to slide.

Outside was also dangerous as ash and pieces of rock rained down. Pliny and the group of terrified people tied pillows to their heads and set out back to the ships in a shower of rocks. Elsewhere it was daybreak, but here was darkness thicker and
20 blacker than any night. By the light of their torches, they succeeded in reaching the ships. But the water was so rough and thick with debris that they could not sail.

PLINY THE YOUNGER

Learning tip

Do you know how to make a sheet of paper look old? Dab the paper with a used, wet teabag. Make sure you have written on the paper before staining it!

Stretch zone

Pliny the Younger wrote this letter 25 years after the eruption. Recall and write about an event that happened in your life five years ago. How clearly can you remember all the details?

Comprehension

A

1 What did Pliny the Elder hope to achieve by making the dangerous journey to Mount Vesuvius during the eruption?

2 What changes did the men observe as they got closer to the land?

B

1 How does Pliny the Younger use language to let the reader know that it was extremely dark?

2 What is Pliny the Younger referring to in the metaphor of 'Broad sheets of brilliant flame'? (lines 11–12)

Volcanoes in art

Many artists have tried to capture the violence and force of a volcano erupting. Below are two examples, one by a Norwegian painter, Johan Christian Dahl, and one by an English artist, Joseph Wright of Derby. Joseph Wright painted over 30 paintings of Mount Vesuvius after he saw an eruption in 1773–5. He was fascinated by the dramatic and colourful effects of fire at night, and used the subject of a volcano erupting to experiment with light effects.

Talk about ...

Pliny the Younger's uncle was in danger as a result of getting close to a volcano. Do you think the painters of these two paintings were in jeopardy as well? Explain your answer.

Eruption of Vesuvius by Johan Christian Dahl, painted in 1824

Vesuvius from Portici by Joseph Wright of Derby, painted in 1774–1776

- Give own opinions clearly and confidently
- Use clues in a picture to answer questions

The next picture is very different. It is a print of Mount Fuji by the Japanese artist, Katsushika Hokusai.

Mount Fuji, which last erupted in 1707, is a Japanese mountain which is famous for its almost perfect cone shape. When conditions are right, in late summer or early autumn, with a wind from the south and a clear sky, the slopes of Mount Fuji can appear red from the rays of the sun.

South Wind, Clear Sky (also known as *Red Fuji*), a woodblock print from 1830–1832 by Katsushika Hokusai

Comprehension

1 Describe what is happening in each of the three paintings (one above and two on page 73).

1 Describe the colours and atmosphere of each of the three paintings.

2 What effect does the presence of people near the lava have in the first painting?

1 Which painting do you like best? Explain your reasons.

Language tip

When you are focusing on describing one particular thing in detail, you often need to make use of a wide range of synonyms.

Synonyms are words that have the same, or nearly the same, meaning.

For example, in describing volcanoes, you might need a range of synonyms to express the great power of an eruption, such as: 'terrible', 'fearful', or 'awe-inspiring'.

Be a radio reporter

You are going to write a radio report about witnessing an eruption of Mount Vesuvius. As you are one of the first reporters at the scene, you will need to describe what you can see and explain what is happening for the listeners. Make the facts sound exciting for an audience who cannot see the scene and have to rely on the description you are giving them to picture it.

- Write several pairs of facts and descriptions to help you draft the report. Use the new vocabulary you have learned in this unit.
- Make sure your report is clearly worded. Aim to include plenty of factual detail and vivid descriptions.
- Read your report aloud, or record it to hear how it sounds. Practise the way you say it out loud to make it sound exciting.
- Use direct and indirect speech to report what other experts and witnesses have to say about it.

- Plan, write and proofread a fictional news report for the radio using suitable vocabulary
- Use speech marks correctly
- Understand the difference between facts and opinions

Learning tip
Remember the difference between fact and description, for example:

Fact: 'Hot lava flows down the side of the volcano.'

Description: 'The lava is like a red river of burning rocks. The heat and smoke is so intense, it is impossible to get close to it.'

Fires at Mount Vesuvius in July 2017

What causes earthquakes and tsunamis?

How much do you know about what causes earthquakes? When one of the Earth's plates slips under another at a plate boundary, it can create an earthquake. These plate boundaries are called fault lines. Cities built on fault lines are at risk of earthquakes.

When an earthquake occurs under the ocean, the tremendous energy of the earthquake is transferred to the water. Waves travel under the ocean faster than a jet plane. These waves can be hundreds of miles long and over ten metres high. When they reach the shore, the effect is a devastating tsunami.

This is what happened on 26 December 2004, when a gigantic earthquake occurred underwater, off the coast of Sumatra in Indonesia. It caused a tsunami which covered 600 kilometres in 75 minutes. The tsunami caused devastation. A great many people lost their lives, and many communities were destroyed across South East Asia.

- Read a non-fiction text and discuss its features
- Think about where words come from
- Work out the meaning of words by looking at their context

Word origins

tsunami (n), a Japanese word made up of *tsu,* meaning 'harbour' and *nami,* meaning 'wave'

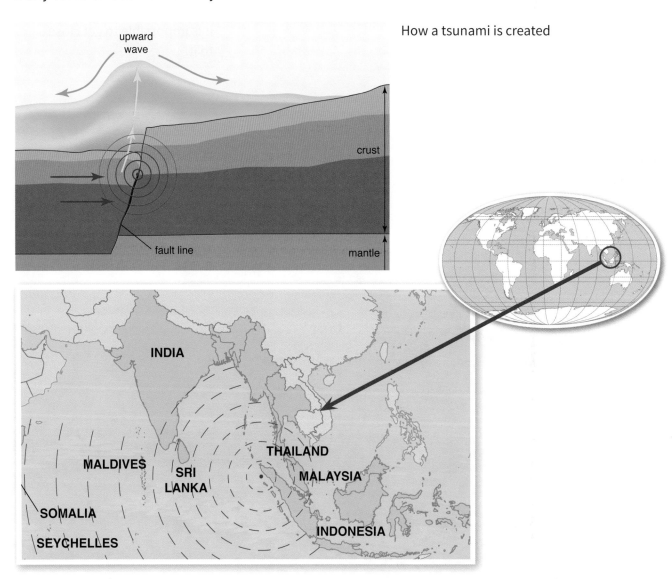

How a tsunami is created

Map of the region most affected by the 2004 tsunami, showing the epicentre of the earthquake

Interpreting images

Image 1 was created by the same Japanese artist who made the print of Mount Fuji that you looked at on page 74. You can see Mount Fuji in the background, but the main part of the picture is a giant wave, or tsunami, in Kanagawa in Japan.

Image 2 is a journalistic photograph showing the devastation caused by the 2004 tsunami and its impact on people's lives.

Journalists often take upsetting photographs that create an emotional response when people see them. What do you think of this method of journalism? How ethical is it to show photographs of people suffering? What does it achieve?

The Great Wave off Kanagawa by Katsushika Hokusai (1831)

Scene of devastation following the 2004 tsunami

Comprehension

 A

1 What do you see in these two images? How do they make you feel?

 B

1 Think of a metaphor and a simile to describe the scene in each of these images.

 C

1 What do you think the artist and the photographer were hoping to achieve when they made these images?

- Compare non-fiction texts
- Work out the meaning of unfamiliar words by looking at them in context
- Explore how setting and character are developed

A story about an amazing elephant

The following text is the true story of Ningnong. She is an elephant who used to give rides to children on one of the beaches hit by the tsunami in Thailand in 2004. As you read the extract, think about how this account of a natural disaster compares to the others you have read in this unit.

Ningnong's great day

Yong was very proud of his young she-elephant, Ningnong. She was strong and good-tempered and never tired of her work. Every morning Yong rose early and rode Ningnong down to the beach. This was Yong's favourite time of day as he watched
5 the waves breaking on the white sand, and breathed in the beauty of the place he loved. The tourists had not yet arrived, and the beach belonged to Yong and his elephant.

On this morning, 26 December 2004, Yong had no idea of the catastrophe which would soon engulf far more than the coast
10 of Thailand. He did not know, either, that not far away the elephants at a tourist centre had spent a restless night, pulling at their chains. Oblivious to all this, Yong watched the birds swirling over the turquoise water in the bay until he heard the excited cries of the children as the first tourists arrived on the
15 beach. Soon a child would ask for a ride on the elephant, and Ningnong's working day would begin.

The day went on like any other day as Ningnong plodded up and down the hot sand and splashed through the shallow water with children on her back. Yong did not know that at the
20 tourist centre above the beach, the elephants had succeeded in breaking their chains and had run up the hill away from the beach. The owners knew something was wrong, and along with some Japanese tourists, they had followed the elephants inland away from the beach.

25 Suddenly Yong became aware that something strange was happening. The water was disappearing. It seemed as though some gigantic force was sucking it away. The tourists had noticed it, too. Some were running away up the beach, and some ran down the beach to see what was happening. Ningnong
30 started to stamp her great feet and make strange noises. Suddenly the air was filled with a low roaring noise. As it grew louder,

Talk about ...

Make sure you understand what these words mean as you read the story. Look them up in a dictionary if you need to.

- to engulf (line 9)
- restless (line 11)
- oblivious (line 12)
- to plod (line 17)
- gigantic (line 27)

- Compare non-fiction texts
- Work out the meaning of unfamiliar words by looking at them in context
- Explore how setting and character are developed

Ningnong pulled at her ropes. In horror and disbelief, people stared at the wall of water which was approaching the beach. How could any wave be that vast? And how could it travel 35 so fast?

There was panic all around Yong. People were shouting and screaming and trying to run with children in their arms. Yong held tight onto the terrified child already riding with him as Ningnong tried to break into a run. Another little girl stood 40 at Ningnong's feet, screaming in terror.

"Oom kun!" ("Pick up!") cried Yong.

Ningnong lifted up the child with her trunk, and having placed her beside Yong, she broke into a run. She raced up the beach and the hillside to safety. Unlike hundreds of people on the 45 beach that day, she and her riders escaped the deadly tsunami which caused such terrible devastation.

- Use clues in a story to answer questions
- Write and then act out a role-play script using suitable vocabulary, grammar and format for a playscript

Comprehension

A

1 Why do you think early morning was Yong's favourite time of day?

2 What two things did Yong do once he saw a wall of water approaching ?

B

1 Write down a synonym for 'engulf'. (line 9)

2 Read the following sentence: 'Ningnong plodded up and down the hot sand'. (lines 17–18) What other words or phrases could replace the word 'plodded'?

C

1 Explain what you think the people were thinking and feeling when they stared 'in horror and disbelief'. (line 32)

Role-playing an interview

Work in groups to produce a role-play based on the story of Yong and the tsunami. One of you will play the part of Yong, and another the girl who was saved. Someone will play the role of a journalist recording interviews for a television news programme. Other members of the group will take the role of local people and tourists who witnessed the tsunami. The journalist should interview a few people to get a variety of eye-witness accounts.

- If you are playing the part of the journalist, prepare questions to ask people.

- If you are playing any of the other parts, re-read the story to remember details and to get an understanding of how the onlookers felt.

- When you carry out the interview, you can use details from the text or make up extra information that fits the story.

- Once you have practised asking and answering your questions, act out your interview for the rest of the class.

Write a TV news documentary

In the months or years after a natural disaster such as the eruption of a volcano, an earthquake, or a tsunami, you can often watch a TV documentary about the events. A documentary is a film that explores real facts and events, and includes photographs, short video clips and interviews with people to present a detailed account of events as they happened and the impact they had on people's lives.

You are going to write a script for a TV news documentary about the effects of tsunamis on people. You may also want to focus on the rescue missions which took place.

In small groups, discuss what features you need to include in your script.

- What tense will it be in?
- Will it be formal or informal style?
- Will you use the first, second or third person?
- Discuss ideas for vocabulary to include.
- Discuss ideas for descriptive language.
- Decide what props you will need, such as pictures or video clips. Will you include reports from experts?

Plan your documentary, proofread it and make improvements. Then practise your performance before taking turns to present your TV documentary to the rest of the class.

Complete this word search

See how many words connected to the topic in this unit you can find in this word search grid. Write down all the words you find in your notebook.

E	A	R	T	H	Q	U	A	K	E
R	C	V	O	S	C	R	U	S	T
U	O	L	A	C	T	I	V	E	U
P	L	A	V	O	S	B	B	C	R
T	L	V	O	N	U	R	N	C	Q
I	I	A	L	E	N	I	A	R	U
O	D	E	C	M	A	G	M	A	O
N	E	F	A	L	M	M	G	T	I
P	V	E	N	T	I	T	H	E	S
A	T	M	O	S	P	H	E	R	E

- Choose an appropriate register for speaking
- Write a TV news documentary
- Use correct grammatical language
- Include suitable vocabulary and vary the sentence types
- Perform a role-play

Language tip
You can make your sentences more interesting by including suitable **conjunctions**, such as those of time (such as 'immediately'), of summary (such as 'in general'), or of place (such as 'near by').

Learning tip
Swap your work with another group's and check for mistakes. Give them helpful, constructive feedback so that they, and you, can make improvements.

Many people and animals help in the rescue missions after natural disasters

How can we make sure that there is enough food for everyone?

> **'** Give me a fish and I eat for a day; teach me to fish and I eat for a lifetime. **'**
>
> Chinese proverb

Talk about ...
- What do you think this Chinese proverb means?
- What is it like not to have enough food?
- Why do you think some people in the world do not have enough to eat?

The world we live in has abundant and varied things for people to eat. There are thousands upon thousands of fruits, vegetables, meats, fish, spices, herbs and grains which humans enjoy eating and which contribute towards their nutrition.

Many people work hard to farm the land, tend to livestock and fish the seas, yet the world does not manage to provide enough food for everyone. You will consider this inequality further later on in this unit.

Word origins

food (n), from the Old English *foda*, meaning 'fuel, nourishment'

nutrition (n), from the Latin *nutrire*, meaning 'to feed or to nourish'

Related words:
- nutritious
- nutritional
- nutrient

Portrait of the Week

This elaborate picture was painted by an Italian artist, Giuseppe Arcimboldo, in 1573. He has created something that is part portrait, and part still-life painting! At first our minds are deceived into thinking it's a face. How many fruits, vegetables and other foods can you see in it? Do you like this painting? Discuss in small groups. Do you all have the same opinions, or do some of you disagree?

Read one person's imaginative description of this painting below. It was written for a series called 'Portrait of the Week' in a newspaper.

- Give own views and question views of others
- Understand how literary devices can make writing interesting

Glossary

proverb short statement that expresses a wise truth

still life arrangement of objects in a painting

eerie strange, mysterious and frightening

rite special ceremony or ritual

Summer by Giuseppe Arcimboldo

This is someone and no one. The dark space of his eyes reveals an emptiness within his shell of summer fruits that is disconcerting and eerie ... Constructed of wheat, figs, plums, pomegranates, peaches, pears and melon, this is like an image from a folk song or sinister tale – the king of summer whose fate is to be burnt at the end of August in some savage rite.

JONATHAN JONES, *The Guardian*, 'Portrait of the Week No. 72'

 Stretch zone

What words and phrases would you use to describe the painting? Write down your ideas. Use your imagination.

Let's compare paintings

* Give own views and question the views of others

Study the still-life paintings shown on this page and page 85. The first was painted by Dutch artist Floris van Dijck in 1615–20. The second, by French artist Paul Cézanne, was painted in 1888–1890. In the seventeenth century, the still-life tradition in the Netherlands focused on the fragility of earthly life and how things do not last forever. Later paintings, such as the one shown by Cézanne, are more a celebration of the fruits of the harvest and of country life.

Still Life with Cheeses by Floris van Dijck

 Stretch zone

* What are the differences in the painting style and the way the food and objects are arranged in both paintings?
* What is similar about them?

- Write a piece of descriptive prose
- Use literary devices to make writing interesting

Kitchen table (Still-life with basket) by Paul Cézanne

Now it's your turn to write about a painting

Re-read the 'Portrait of the Week' about Arcimboldo's *Summer* on page 83. You are now going to write about your own 'Painting of the Week'. Choose one of the paintings illustrated on these pages and write a paragraph about it. Begin with a catchy phrase, as if you are writing a story. Include all of the following points:

- Describe the painted scene in vivid detail.
- How life-like is the scene?
- Do you feel like you are part of the picture?
- What is the overall mood of the painting?

Language tip

Nouns can be modified with additional words placed before or after the noun. These **noun phrases** can include additional nouns, adverbs and adjectives to provide descriptive detail and emotional expression.

Examples from 'Portrait of the Week' on page 83:

- 'The dark space of his eyes'
- 'his shell of summer fruits'

- Contribute to a discussion and share own ideas
- Discuss the context and setting of a story

What is it like not to have enough to eat?

Look at this photograph of people picking over a rubbish heap, searching for anything that could be used or sold for food.

Talk about ...

- What do you think has happened to make these people look through a rubbish heap?
- How can people in cities be short of food?

It is usually animals that *forage*, or search for food, but when people are desperately hungry, they too forage in rubbish bins or anywhere they may find something edible. What do you think life must be like for these people?

An old story set in Korea

The following text comes from a story set in a village in Korea in the twelfth century. What do you imagine life must have been like then? Tree-ear is a 12-year-old boy who shares a shelter under a bridge with Crane-man, a kindly old man who has looked after Tree-ear since he was a very young orphan. He called Tree-ear by that name because he was an orphan and had no parents, just like tree-ear, a wrinkly fungus which seems to emerge straight from rotten wood. Both Crane-man and Tree-ear are constantly hungry and survive on what they can forage.

Tree-ear fungus

- Read a range of texts and express opinions
- Discuss the context and setting of a story

A lucky day

Tree-ear was setting off in the early morning to forage in the village rubbish heaps. Ahead of him a man carried a heavy load on a jiggeh, an open-framed backpack made of branches. On the jiggeh was a large container made of woven straw, the
5 kind commonly used to carry rice.

Tree-ear knew that the rice must be from last-year's crop; in the fields surrounding the village this season's rice had only just begun to grow. It would be many months before the rice was harvested and the poor people allowed to glean the fallen
10 grain from the bare fields. Only then would they taste the rice and feel its solid goodness in their bellies. Just looking at the man's backpack made Tree-ear even hungrier.

Then, as Tree-ear stared, rice began to trickle out. The trickle thickened and became a stream. Oblivious to the hole in his
15 straw container, the man continued on his way.

For a few short moments Tree-ear's thoughts wrestled with one another. Tell him – quickly! Before he loses too much. No! Don't say anything – you will be able to pick up the fallen rice after he rounds the bend …

20 Tree-ear made his decision. He waited until the man had reached the bend in the road, then ran to catch him up.

"Honourable sir," Tree-ear said, panting and bowing. "As I walked behind you, I noticed that you are losing rice from your jiggeh!"

25 The farmer turned and saw the trail of rice. He pushed his straw hat back, scratched his head, and laughed ruefully.

"Impatience!" said the farmer. "I should have had a double wall in this container. But it would have taken more time. Now I am paying for not having waited a little longer."

30 He struggled out of the jiggeh's straps and inspected the container. He prodded the straw to close the gap, but without success.

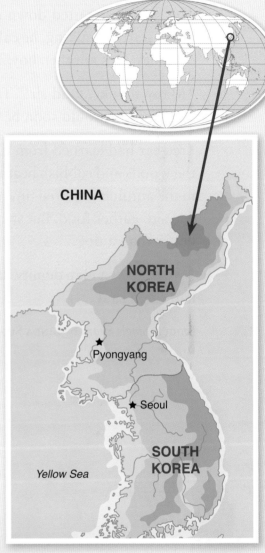

CHINA

NORTH KOREA

★ Pyongyang

★ Seoul

SOUTH KOREA

Yellow Sea

Map showing the location of North and South Korea

Glossary

glean pick up grain left behind by harvesters

"Fetch me a few leaves, boy," said the farmer. Tree-ear did so, and the man stuffed them into the container as a temporary
35 patch.

The farmer squatted down to load the jiggeh onto his back. As he started walking, he called over his shoulder. "One good deed deserves another, boy. The rice on the ground is yours."

"Many thanks, kind sir!" Tree-ear bowed, very pleased. His
40 waist-pouch would soon be filled with rice.

?

What responsibility do people with enough food have towards those who do not have enough?

Tree-ear had learned from Crane-man's example. Foraging in the woods and rubbish heaps and gathering fallen grain-heads in the autumn required time and work. They were honourable ways to gather food. But stealing and begging made a man no
45 better than a dog.

"Work gives a man dignity, stealing takes it away," Crane-man had often said.

From *A Single Shard* by LINDA SUE PARK

- Work out the meaning of words by looking at the context
- Summarize a text and understand its purpose

Comprehension

A 👤

1 What is the pack on the man's back made of?
2 Why are poor people like Tree-ear hungry at this time of year?
3 How is the man 'paying for not having waited a little longer'? (line 29)
4 What does the saying 'One good deed deserves another' mean? (lines 37–38)
5 According to Tree-ear, what is the difference between 'foraging' and 'stealing'?

B 👤

1 After Tree-ear sees the rice pouring out from the man's backpack, his thoughts 'wrestled with one another'. What does this mean? (lines 16–17)
2 What is a 'temporary patch'? How does the man make it? (lines 34–35)
3 Which words tell you that Tree-ear is respectful towards the man carrying the rice?
4 Think of a synonym you could use for 'ruefully'. (line 26)

C 👥

1 What lessons do you think Tree-ear learns from his experience?
2 What does Crane-man mean when he says, "Work gives a man dignity, stealing takes it away"? (line 46) Do you agree with him?

How do people try to help others?

There are many ways of helping those who are hungry and homeless. Most people donate money and others volunteer their time. Some people set up organizations to give help and support to those who need it. One Acre Fund is a non-profit social enterprise based in Africa which provides training and financial support to smallholders to help them 'grow their way out of hunger' and farm in a sustainable way that benefits both producers and consumers.

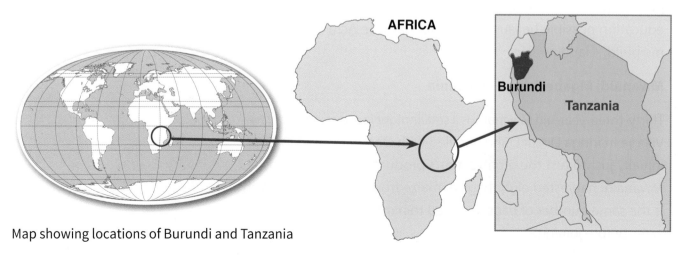

Map showing locations of Burundi and Tanzania

Celebrating women farmers: the backbone of Africa's rural agriculture

Women farmers tend to invest more in their homes and families, thereby fuelling the prosperity of their communities. In fact, the UN's Food and Agriculture Organization estimates that if women smallholders had the same access to productive resources as men,
5   they could increase food production by 30% and reduce world hunger by 15%. We spoke to several farmers in our program to find out how they feel about their experience farming with One Acre Fund.

Claudine Manirankunda, Giheta – Burundi

10   When 29-year-old Claudine joined One Acre Fund Burundi in 2015, she found it extremely taxing because she found the pre-planting process long and exhausting. But, as time went by, she saw how healthy her crops looked, which inspired her. "When it was time to harvest, I was astonished by the results. The same land that used to
15   yield 50 kg gave me 300 kg of beans. I even harvested half a ton of maize during the last season. For the first time in my life, I was making a profit.

"When I got married, I didn't know how to be a provider for my family. My husband works in the city, and I was supposed to care
20   for his land with little agricultural knowledge. Since joining One Acre Fund, my anxiety has disappeared. Not only did One Acre Fund give me the knowledge I needed, but they also empowered me to become more self-assured about my place in the household. Today, my family lives very comfortably. I can also dream big and envision
25   things like owning cattle and building a bigger home. My daughter just started school, and I know I will be able to give her the best education possible because of the life that One Acre Fund helped me build," Claudine says.

Mwanaidi Mgabe, Iringa - Tanzania

30   Thirty-three-year-old Mwanaidi is a smallholder farmer from Kitayawa Village in Iringa District. She enrolled with One Acre Fund in 2017, initially just to test the organization's products. In the first season, Mwanaidi harvested eight bags of maize from half an acre, which is the same number of bags she used to harvest on one and a half
35   acres before joining.

Glossary

one acre almost half a hectare

enterprise business or company

smallholders people who own small plots of agricultural land

productive able to produce large amounts of food

envision imagine

empowered feeling more confident

self-assured confident in your own abilities

sustainable can be kept at a certain level

- Read a non-fiction text and discuss its features
- Use clues in a text to answer questions
- Understand the purpose of a text
- Give own views and question views of others

"I love how we are trained to harvest by cutting the maize stalks and arranging them in a pile; this way, I harvest all my maize without leaving any in the field," Mwanaidi says. From her surplus, Mwanaidi has fixed a door for her new house and purchased iron sheets for her kitchen.

40

Women are central to agriculture, and a central part of our work. By opening up new opportunities for them, we are helping farming women develop new, sustainable incomes to build lasting livelihoods.

Comprehension

 A

1 What challenges has the One Acre Fund helped Claudine to overcome?

2 What training did Mwanaidi find particularly helpful? How did this help her with farming her crops?

3 What other practical benefits has this had for Mwanaidi?

 B

1 What does Claudine mean when she says she can 'dream big'? (line 24)

2 Find words and phrases in the text which show how the One Acre Fund has changed the lives of female farmers. Explain how this affects the reader's opinion of the Fund's work.

3 What is the purpose of this text?

 C

1 Reread the final paragraph. To what extent do you agree?

2 Think of some other ways the One Acre Fund could support sustainable farming in Africa and around the world.

3 Do you know about a charitable organization which helps people in your country? What kind of work does it do?

- Summarize a text and understand its purpose
- Compare non-fiction texts

Eco-holiday advertisement

While lots of people go on holiday to relax, some go to work! Would you like to go on the holiday advertised below?

CALLING ALL ECO-ADVENTURERS!

The adventure of a lifetime awaits you in the mountains of the Brazilian Atlantic Forest! Here at Eco Fazenda Estrela, we are committed to adopting sustainable farming practices which will regenerate and restore exhausted, over-farmed land. Join our hard-working team for a volunteering holiday and learn all you need to know about eco-farming, permaculture and bioconstruction.

We can't wait to meet you! Até logo!

Glossary

fazenda 'farm' in Portuguese
estrela 'star' in Portuguese
regenerate bring new life to an area
permaculture low input/high productivity farming system
bioconstruction construction using living organisms

David's eco-holiday diary

David, who is from London, went on one of the Eco Fazenda Estrela volunteer holidays and the following is an extract from the diary he wrote describing his first two days.

Wednesday, February 16th

We arrived late last night in a jeep which bumped its way along rough, mud tracks. After a night's sleep and breakfast overlooking the beautiful forest we were ready for work. And what work! I can hardly lift my pen to write. All day long we've been clearing an area ready for planting and sowing. This involved cutting undergrowth with a machete, and carting away barrow loads of sand and earth. We think we work hard in the office, but this is real work.

Thursday, February 17th

Today we heaved bag after bag after bag of manure into the earth. I lost count of how many. We were warned against the little brown spiders on the forest floor, which are lethal. A bite would kill you so, despite the heat, we made sure our trousers were tucked into our boots. I slipped and fell in the mud over and over again, but we all laughed each time. I'm sure the muscles in my arms are bigger than they were yesterday but I have blisters on my hands. I'm exhausted, but it's rewarding to know that all my hard work will help local people to grow fruit and vegetables which are sustainable and, most importantly, delicious!

⊙ Stretch zone

When you have finished reading David's diary, go back and review any words you didn't understand. Examine each of the words in its context in the sentence. Write down what you think the definition for that word is, then check in a dictionary to see if you were correct.

- Use clues in a text to answer questions
- Understand how a text can be written to persuade you
- Consider how different grammatical features create meaning and organize ideas
- Write a diary entry
- Plan, proofread and correct writing

Comprehension

 A

1 What words let you know that David was very tired after his first day?

2 Why did David tuck his trousers into his boots?

3 How do you know that, despite working very hard, David was enjoying himself?

 B

1 What is the purpose of this text?

2 Who do you think David is writing his diary to?

3 Words are used in David's diary to create a dramatic effect. Find three examples and explain the effect they give.

4 Which words or phrases in the advertisement are aimed at persuading people like David to volunteer? Explain the effect each of these has.

 C

1 What different feelings and emotions has David experienced in his first two days on the tour?

2 How do you think he will feel when the tour ends in a week's time?

Now it's your turn to write a diary

David's eco-holiday continued for another week, and included two rest days on a local beach. He kept a diary throughout to remind him of what he did and to reflect on what was being achieved.

- Imagine that you are David on the eco-holiday.
- Write reflective diary entries for three more days from his eco-holiday.
- Make a list of all the steps you need to go through when writing. You can look back at the list as you plan and write.
- Use information from the article about the One Acre Fund on pages 90–91 to give you further ideas about eco-agricultural activities David might participate in, and make up additional activities yourself.

 ?

Talk about any people in your local area who are disadvantaged for some reason. In what ways could you and your classmates help these people?

Language tip
You use the first-person singular and plural pronouns when you write a diary.

First-person pronouns include the speaker: 'I', 'we', 'us', 'our', 'my'.

- Identify and discuss ideas in poems
- Explore how setting and character are developed
- Discuss the context and setting of a poem
- Learn new vocabulary by reading a variety of poems

An African poem

In some parts of the world, food is harder to grow than in others. Where resources are scarce, providing food for even one family can be hard work. The following poem is about the life of an African woman from Malawi who works hard to provide for her family.

Why the Old Woman Limps

Do you know why the old woman sings?
She is sixty years old with six grandchildren to look after
While her sons and wives are gone south to dig gold.
Each day she milks the goat, sells the milk to buy soap,
5 Feeds and washes the children, and tethers the goat.
In the evening she tells them all stories of old at the
fireside:
I know why the old woman sings.

Do you know when the old woman sleeps?
10 She rests with the dark, at night she thinks of
Tomorrow: she's to feed the children and graze the goat.
She's to weed the garden, water the seedling beans,
The thatch has to be mended, the barnyard cleared.
Maize pounded, chaff winnowed, millet ground, fire lit …
15 I do not know when the old woman sleeps.

Do you know why the old woman limps?
She goes to fetch water in the morning
and the well is five miles away,
Goes to fetch firewood with her axe
20 and the forest is five miles the other way,
Goes to the fields to look for pumpkin leaves
leaving the goat tethered to the well tree
And hurries home to the children to cook:
I know why the old woman limps.

LUPENGA MPHANDE

Glossary

thatch roof covering made of dried grasses, palm leaves or reeds

chaff winnowed husks (inedible seed cases) have to be separated or 'winnowed' from the grain or seeds before making flour

Malawi is in south-east Africa

Comprehension

A

1 Who is the woman looking after and providing food for?
2 What kind of work does she do?
3 Which of her tasks would you least like to do? Give your reasons.
4 Explain in your own words why the woman's sons and their wives have gone.
5 How important is the goat to the woman and her family?

B

1 To whom do you think the questions in the poem are addressed?
2 What are 'stories of old'? (line 6)
3 Think of synonyms for 'graze' and 'tethered'. (lines 11 and 22)
4 What is the effect of listing some of the work that the old woman does? (lines 4, 5, 11, 12, 13, 14)
5 What effect does missing out the pronoun in the third stanza have?

C

1 Talk about the three questions (in the first line of each stanza) in the poem. What answers can you suggest?

Now it's your turn to be a poet

Make a list of the things you have to do each day after you wake up. Write your own poem starting with the words: 'Do you know why …?' Start your final line with the words: 'I know why …' Use the poem 'Why the Old Woman Limps' as a model. Your poem does not have to rhyme!

Talk about …

- What does the woman have to do each day after she wakes up?
- What do you have to do?
- What do these tasks reveal about your life compared to hers?

- Learn new vocabulary by reading different stories
- Explore how setting and character are developed

Read a Chinese fairytale

This Chinese fairytale offers further insights into how eating and preparing food is central to our desire for a happy home life. It tells the story of Hsieh Tuan and his struggles to find a wife who can help him cook and tidy the house.

The Dinner that Cooked Itself

Tuan was a tall, handsome youth of 18. He was only a humble clerk in the magistrate's court, but he worked always with a will, and his honesty and respectful bearing impressed all who knew him. His father and mother had both died when he was
5 very small, but a kind neighbour, old Wang, had taken him in and treated him as one of his own sons. Now that Tuan had reached manhood he moved into a little house of his own. Not far from the house he had a small strip of land, where he tended his rice-plants and beans each day when his duties at court
10 were done.

It was old Wang who hired a go-between to seek out a wife for Tuan. The go-between suggested Miss Ch'en, the pretty daughter of a farmer on the outskirts of the town.

But when the dates of birth were compared, it was found that
15 Miss Ch'en had been born in the year of the cat. Now Tuan belonged to the year of the dog; and with cat and dog under one roof there would never be a day's peace in the house. [...]

One match after another was considered and rejected. Even when everything else was right, people would object that Tuan
20 was too poor to marry their daughter. But none of this made any difference to Tuan's daily work, which began at cock-crow when he left for the magistrate's court, and ended at nightfall when he returned from cultivating his tiny field.

One night Tuan, his hoe over his shoulder, was making his way
25 slowly along the narrow path which joined his field to his house. [...] He looked down to follow the winding of the narrow path. The moonlight glimmered on a stone by the edge of the path at his feet. But the stone had never been there before. And was it really a stone after all? It was rounded, and pointed at
30 the top. He bent down for a closer look. Not a stone, but a snail – an enormous, giant snail, quite the size of a small bucket.

Glossary

fairytale story about imaginary beings and lands

go-between someone who helps people to meet, or arranges a marriage

cock-crow very early in the morning when a rooster crows

hoe tool for breaking up soil, and scraping off weeds

- Learn new vocabulary by reading different stories
- Explore how setting and character are developed

Of course, it was a sign of great good luck to find such a <u>rarity</u>. Delighted, Tuan raised the snail gently in his hands and hurried on home. On the way he picked some succulent leaves for it
35 to eat, and these he put together with the snail in a large, roomy <u>earthenware</u> storage-jar which stood just inside his door. He went to bed still rejoicing over his good fortune. In the morning when he woke, his first thought was to look inside the jar, and he was pleased to see that the snail had eaten a hearty breakfast.

40 And now a very curious thing happened. Tuan went off to the court as usual and came back home in the afternoon to have a bite to eat before going out to his field. But when he entered his little house he found the table set with bowl and chopsticks. Steam rose temptingly from a dish of cooked rice and vegetables,
45 and on the newly swept floor was his large washing-bowl, filled with hot water ready for him to use!

"How kind people are," Tuan thought as he washed his hands and face and <u>squatted</u> down to attack his dinner. "It must be Mrs Wang who has stolen in here secretly to give me such a
50 pleasant surprise. What a thoughtful thing to do!"

Never in his life had he tasted such delicious cooking. As soon as he had washed up he hurried to Mrs Wang's house to thank her. But he was mistaken. Mrs Wang had not been near his cottage, and could not imagine who it might have been. [...]

55 Every day for over a week the same thing went on happening. Each day Tuan would come home to find his room swept, his washing-water all heated and ready and his dinner waiting on the table. The news spread
60 among all the neighbours, but no one offered to explain the mystery. At last Tuan determined to get to the bottom of it. He left his house as usual at the first crow of the cock. But as soon as
65 the sun was up he came secretly back, and hid outside the fence to watch what might happen in the house.

Glossary

succulent juicy and tasty
hearty large and nourishing

- Learn new vocabulary by reading different stories
- Explore how setting and character are developed

For a while all was still. Then, suddenly, there was a movement:
through the doorway he saw a hand appear out of the huge
65 earthenware jar. After the hand another hand; and a lovely
young girl, beautifully dressed in a silk robe, climbed out of
the jar and crossed the room to the stove in the corner.

Quickly Tuan left his hiding-place and entered the house. His
first concern was to look inside the jar – no snail was there,
70 but only an empty shell! In the corner by the stove the girl
pressed herself against the wall in alarm.

"Who are you?" asked Tuan. "Where do you come from, and
why are you looking after my house for me?"

The girl said nothing. Her frightened glance darted about the
75 room, and she tried to dash across to the earthenware jar, but
Tuan prevented her.

Finally she spoke. Her voice was clear and sweet like a <u>tinkling</u>
of jades. "I am a fairy," she said, "and my name is White Wave.
The Lord of Heaven took pity on you because you are an
80 orphan and live alone. And because you work hard and are
honest and polite, he sent me to look after you. I was to stay
with you for ten years, until you grew rich and married a wife.
Then I was to leave you and return to Fairyland. But now you
have <u>spied</u> on me in secret, and you have seen my true form.
85 This is not permitted to a mortal. I must leave you at once.
You must continue to work hard at court and cultivate your
land with all your strength. But you may keep the shell which
I left in the jar. Use it for storing rice, and empty it only when
hunger threatens. You will find that it will at once fill up again."

Jade pendant in the shape of a mythical creature

90 In vain Tuan pleaded with her to stay. No effort would succeed;
she had to go. [...]

From that time onwards he was never short of food. And
although he never became <u>outstandingly</u> wealthy, he married
a wife who at last made him very happy all his life.

From *Tales from China* by Cyril Birch

Comprehension

A

1 What obstacles are there to Tuan finding a wife?

2 Why would Tuan make a good husband?

3 Who is the snail, and why does she stay at Tuan's house? Why does she leave?

4 How does the shell continue to be of help to Tuan?

B

1 Match each of the words underlined in the story with the correct definition below using its context to help you.

   a pottery made from clay

   b observed secretly

   c using land for crops

   d a light ringing sound

   e where criminals have their offence judged

   f sat with knees bent

   g of low importance

   h no longer a child

   i doesn't happen very often

   j exceptionally

2 Find some examples of words and short phrases chosen by the writer that let the reader know that unusual events have taken place.

C

1 According to the story, what does a person need for a happy life? Do you agree?

- Work out the meaning of unknown words by looking at them in context
- Discuss the context and setting of a story
- Explore a character's point of view through role-play

 Stretch zone

In this extract, the author uses a simile to describe the fairy's voice as 'like a tinkling of jades' (lines 77–78). Jade stone is very important in Chinese culture, and is sometimes called the 'stone of heaven'. When pieces of jade knock together, they make a delicate tinkling sound. In Chinese culture, jade is believed to possess the power to avert evil and bad luck while fostering health and good fortune.

- Find out about other gemstones that have cultural significance.

Getting inside the characters' heads

'The Dinner that Cooked Itself' is written in the third person, so we only know what the characters are thinking and feeling from what the narrator tells us. In small groups, 'hot-seat' the characters of Tuan, the fairy, and Tuan's future wife. Each person should take on the role of one of the characters, and the others will interview them and ask them about their personal opinion and/or experience of the events narrated in the story.

7 Wildlife

How do humans and animals live together?

> 'Everywhere the People of the Sea told him the same things.
>
> Seals had come to these islands once upon a time, but men had killed them all off.'
>
> From 'The White Seal' in *The Jungle Book* by RUDYARD KIPLING

Talk about ...

- What wild animals have you seen? Did you see them in the wild or in a zoo?
- Do you know of any animals, birds or sea creatures in the world which are now endangered?
- Can you think of ways in which people could protect animals?

Rudyard Kipling's 'The White Seal' tells the story of a brave white seal, Kotick, who tries to find a safe place where his fellow seals can live without the fear of being hunted and killed by humans.

In the past, hunters have killed many varieties of seal for their fur, resulting in the extinction of some species. Hunting still remains a threat to seals today, along with decreasing fish supplies and getting caught in fishing nets.

Wild seals are very intelligent and curious, and it is not surprising that they are popular with humans. However, it is now illegal to interfere in any way with seals in many countries, and this includes not only touching them, but also making them change their normal behaviour by approaching them. Do you think laws around the world do enough to protect wildlife from human activity?

Entertainment in Roman times

Have you ever visited the Colosseum in Rome? Do you know why it was built? It is the remains of a gigantic stadium in the capital of the Roman Empire and, two thousand years ago, it could hold 50,000 people. Today, an audience would be there to watch a football match or a pop concert.

Do you know what the people crowded in to see two thousand years ago in Rome? The performances in the Colosseum started in 80 CE. In these performances, skilled fighting men called gladiators fought each other, and also fought wild animals. Lions, bears, panthers and leopards were just some of the animals captured for these popular contests that went on for hundreds of years, and may have had an impact on animal populations.

The remains of the Colosseum in Rome

When animal populations decrease year by year, they eventually become endangered. This means they are in danger of completely dying out and becoming extinct. Both their habitats, the places where they live and feed, and the animals themselves have to be protected.

The relationship between humans and animals is complicated. Many people love to see animals living in their natural habitat, and are concerned about the effects of human activity, but human beings can also place themselves at risk when they encounter wild animals. If you encounter an animal in the wild, it is important not to get too close, not to feed them, scare them, or surprise them if they have young (they will be very protective).

A Roman mosaic of gladiators and a tiger

- Express opinions about a story

A close encounter on a safari walk

The following extract is a personal account of an adventure in an African wildlife park in the Okavango Delta, Botswana. The writer is a guide in the wildlife park.

The guide is approaching the end of a safari walk with his group when an unexpected event puts his skills to the test.

Wild buffalo

At the edge of the plain, a group of zebra was slowly making its way to the shade of the trees. Apart from the zebra, nothing moved as I led my group of tourists forward. They were happy now that the camp was near and they would soon have a cool

5 drink. When we were half way across the plain, I caught a glimpse of a bush some distance away which was shaking. As there was no breeze, I knew an animal must be causing the disturbance. I raised my hand, motioning to the group to stay silent.

10 A buffalo emerged from the bush he had wrecked, obviously in a dangerous mood. With no breeze, he wouldn't smell us, but he'd soon see us. I made slow hand signs, directing the group to squat whilst I kept my eyes on the buffalo. He hadn't spotted us. Then I heard a sound.

15 'Click, whirr, click, whirr.'

I turned round quickly and my eyes confirmed my fears. Jacques, a young member of the group, was standing up taking photos, and the buffalo was now glaring at this new object with his yellow-ringed eyes. The huge animal stepped forward, horns

20 high and nose glistening. I had to make a plan, and make it fast. I looked at the flat plain. We would never make it to the trees, but there was a large termite mound not far away. I waved for the group to follow me to it and whispered for them to wait for me there. The buffalo was slowly moving forward.

25 I started to run across the plain back to where we had come from. Glancing over my shoulder, I saw that the buffalo had taken the bait and was watching me with his nostrils flaring and his head held high. Having reached the grove of trees,

Glossary

taken the bait (*idiom*) react to something that someone has done exactly as they intended

- Use clues in a story to answer questions

I crept silently towards the group of grazing zebra.
30 Suddenly I burst out of my cover, waving my arms and shouting. The zebras ran away, and as they ran, they made a whistling noise which warned other animals of danger. The buffalo, now close to the termite mound where the tourists huddled, heard the zebras' warning whistle. He knew that whatever was
35 pursuing the zebra was a danger to him, too. In an instant, he changed course and ran off in a cloud of dust behind the zebras.

I ran back to the termite mound and collected my frightened group. As we walked back to the camp no one spoke a word to Jacques.

From *Whatever You Do, Don't Run* by PETER ALLISON

Comprehension

A

1 Why is it obvious that the buffalo is in a dangerous mood?
2 What does Jacques do to attract the buffalo's attention?
3 What is the guide's plan to save his group from being approached by the buffalo?
4 Why does the zebras' whistling make the buffalo run?

B

1 'Click, whirr, click, whirr' is an example of what literary device? (line 15)
2 Find a synonym for 'squat'. (line 13)
3 What phrase tells us that the rest of the group was not happy with Jacques?

C

1 Should tourists be allowed to get close to wild animals? Explain your answer.
2 Would you like to go on a safari walk? Give reasons for your answer.

 Stretch zone

Find out if any animals in your country or one nearby are endangered. How endangered are they? Compare your findings with others in the class.

- Read a variety of texts and consider their features
- Understand how texts are structured and organized

Write a dialogue

Write a short dialogue between the guide and Jacques reflecting one part of the event on the previous pages, or a conversation after the event. Perhaps the guide explains to Jacques why everyone is annoyed with him. Write the dialogue like an extract from a play. Use the sample provided to start your dialogue. Look carefully at the punctuation used. When writing a dialogue, you do not use quotation marks as you do when you are writing direct speech. When you are ready, act out your dialogue with a partner.

Safari guide: I'd like to speak to you, Jacques.

Jacques: Sure. Is it about what happened?

Understanding animals

Here is a comic strip that aims to teach people something about wild animals. This strip focuses on their sense of vision. What does the eye position tell you about an animal?

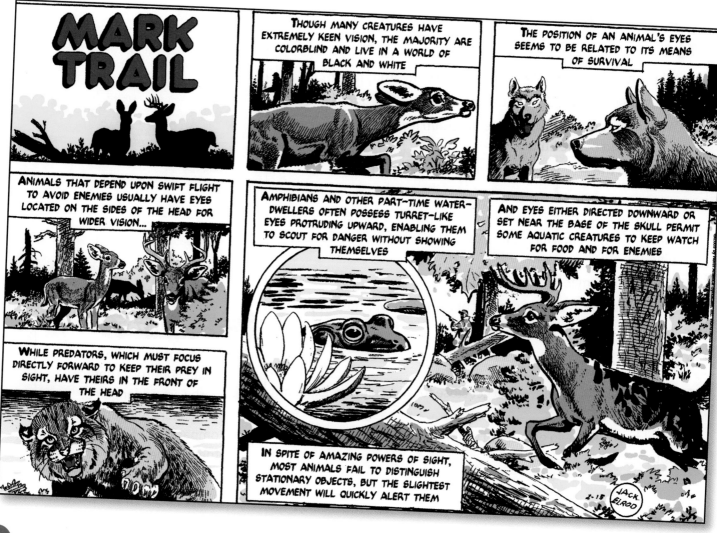

- Write a comic strip
- Use a model text to help with own writing

Making a comic strip

Make your own comic strip about wild animals. You will need to research a particular animal or aspect of animals, such as their sense of smell. Then set out the information with illustrations. You can create your own illustrations on paper, or you can cut and paste printed images from magazines and leaflets. Alternatively, you could work on a computer screen, using images you find on the internet. Whichever method you use, make sure your work looks eye-catching and interesting.

Why is it important for us to understand how animals behave in the wild? Discuss your ideas in small groups.

Here are some suggestions for research topics:

- types of fur or skin for protection
- cold-blooded or warm-blooded creatures
- types of wings
- types of habitats
- animals in extreme climates.

A story about seals

Jenny is on holiday in Greece with her parents and older brother, Joe. They want to visit a tiny rocky island. Jenny explores the island and is very excited when she sees a seal dive into a cave beneath the rocks.

Jenny's secret

I wondered if the cave would have a hole in its roof. And it did. I searched around and I found the opening, half hidden by a little bush. At first when I looked in all I could see was a pattern of shimmering green and gold all over the cave walls.
5 Then I could make out a big cavern with a stony floor and rock shelves. And I was there, looking in, when the seal swam in through the opening and hauled himself out of the water and onto the little beach inside the cave. It was only then that I noticed three more seals lying on rock shelves high up.

10 Two of them had babies. I could hear the little bleating noise from the pups. It was the most magical and beautiful thing I'd ever heard. I realised that for once in my life I knew something that not one of the rest of my family knew. I stood up, and saw that Stefanos was bringing his boat in closer. He was waving
15 at us and shouting that there was a storm coming and we must return. Suddenly clouds came over the sun and I could feel the wind getting stronger. Stefanos kept the boat steady and he and I waited for the others to join us. It was then that he said that he knew what I'd found. He told me it was the last hiding
20 place of that seal family and that if they were disturbed the mothers might abandon their pups, or even kill them. That was why he tried to stop people going there.

"I didn't disturb them!" I cried.

"No, I'm sure you didn't," said Stefanos. "But will you betray them?"

25 He glanced at my parents and Joe packing up on the beach.

"My family wouldn't hurt them."

"But they would want to look, wouldn't they? They would dive down, just once, thinking there could be no harm in that. And later others might hear them talking about what they had
30 seen and come out to see for themselves …"

Talk about …

• What is the best holiday you have ever had? Alternatively, what would be your dream holiday destination?

• Tell the rest of your group about it.

• Ask each other questions.

Language tip

Different types of sentences are used in the extract.

Statement: Two of them had babies.

Exclamation: "I didn't disturb them!"

Question: "But will you betray them?"

- Use clues in a story to answer questions
- Look at words with prefixes
- Write a journal entry

[...] "I'll give you something else to tell them instead," he said. "Hundreds of years ago, people believed that a tent made of sealskin would protect them from lightning." The sky was dark and rain was starting. "Will you tell them that and keep the

35 seals' secret? For the seals' sake?"

And then everyone was climbing on board. The water was choppy and the weather was worsening.

"Someone doesn't mind the weather!" said my father suddenly.

There he was, my seal, his head just above the surface of

40 the water.

"You'd think there would be a whole family of them, wouldn't you?" said my mother.

It was almost unbearable. I said, "I can tell you something none of you know."

45 And I told them about the sealskin tent and lightning. I had kept the seals' secret. It was worth it for the seals – and for the smile Stefanos gave me.

From *Watching* by JUDY ALLEN

Comprehension

 A

1 What is special about the place Jenny finds?

2 What would happen if people came to look at the seals?

3 Why might telling her family about the seals be bad for the seals, even though her family would never want to hurt them?

4 What is the significance of the story about the sealskin?

 B

1 Which verb means 'to leave behind', or 'to desert'? (paragraph 2)

2 What does 'betray' mean? What would happen to the seals if Jenny 'betrayed' them? (line 24)

3 Which adjective towards the end of the text tells you that the water is beginning to get rough?

4 Which word in the text with a prefix of *un-* or *in-* means the same as 'intolerable'?

 C

1 Can you think of any other stories you know where people protect animals and their life in the wild?

Write a journal entry about a holiday

Using all the ideas from the holiday stories you have talked about with your group, write a journal or diary entry about a memorable experience with an animal on a holiday. It can be real or imaginary. Find or draw a picture of the animal to go with your journal entry.

When my family and I were on an adventure holiday in Costa Rica, we encountered a colourful toucan ...

Why is it difficult to protect animals?

Sometimes the interests of human beings and of the animals who live in the same area may be in conflict. There may be good reasons why it is difficult to protect the local wildlife.

Around Vladivostok in Russia, there are uninhabited forests known as *taiga*. For many centuries, the forests have provided a habitat for Siberian tigers where they can live and feed undisturbed by human beings. However, Siberian tigers are now endangered, which means they may become extinct.

- Write grammatically correct sentences with correct punctuation

Glossary

taiga vast areas of forest in Siberia in the Russian Far East

Language tip

Many of the extracts in this unit use an 's' to show belonging (the **possessive**).

These include: 'the zebra's warning whistle' (singular); 'the seals' secret' (plural, with an apostrophe after the 's').

List other examples you find in this unit, and identify if they are singular or plural.

RUSSIA

Vladivostok

ASIA

108

Email to the editor

The letters page of a magazine or newspaper prints letters and email messages sent in by readers to express their thoughts, opinions or strong beliefs. Sometimes a reader's letter or email ends by asking a question, in the hope that someone else will write to supply the answer.

From: Sabine Ketelsen

To: Editor

Subject: Save the Siberian tigers!

Recently I travelled to Vladivostok, where the beautiful Siberian tigers live in the nearby forests. I joined a group tour to see the animals in their natural habitat. I was shocked to learn that since the 1990s the habitat of the Siberian tigers has been taken over more and more by human beings.

Unemployment is high in the area and many people have turned to poaching. These activities are illegal. They are killing animals such as wild boar and deer, which the tigers feed on. Some people are even killing the tigers. A tiger's skin can be sold for as much money as a year's income, and the bones and internal organs are sold for medicine. Although patrols have reduced the number of killings, tigers are still dying.

Life is harsh for the local people, and forests are a good source of income for them; they cut down the trees and transport the logs for sale, sometimes legally and sometimes illegally. But this logging is destroying the tigers' habitat. Both the tigers and the people are struggling to survive.

I have heard that the government is trying to solve the conflicts between humans and animals. But there are only about 350 adult tigers left! I'm wondering what is being done, and if any international organizations are trying to save these amazing creatures?

Sabine Ketelsen, Hamburg

SEND

Language tip
As you read the email, look at the **emotive words** used. Think about how the message would not be as strong if weaker words had been used.

Comprehension

A

1 What is the tigers' habitat?

2 What is happening to the tigers' food supply?

3 Why have some people been killing tigers?

- Understand how texts are structured and organized
- Use clues in a text to answer questions
- Choose an appropriate register to write in
- Write an organized text for a particular purpose
- Use patterns and rules to help you to spell words correctly
- Develop strategies to help you with difficult spellings

Comprehension

1 Is Sabine's email formal or informal? Give some examples from the email to support your answer.

2 Is the email mostly fact or opinion? Give some examples from the email to support your answer.

3 There are two examples in the email where different prefixes have been added to the start of a word to form the opposite. What are these? Find some words in the email that you could add prefixes to in order to form the opposite.

1 Describe Sabine's feelings as she wrote the email.

2 What sort of person do you think Sabine is?

Write your reply

Write an email as the editor in reply to Sabine Ketelsen. Find out which organizations are trying to help save the Siberian tiger, and explain three or four of the things they are doing. Think about what features you will need to include and begin your email with 'Dear Ms Ketelsen'.

Remember that you are the editor of the magazine or newspaper, so take extra care over your spelling and punctuation.

What happens when animals are a threat?

Sometimes it is difficult for wild animals to be protected because they pose a serious danger to people or to their domestic animals.

The events described in the following story happened in South Asia in the 1930s. At that time, tigers regularly killed the cattle belonging to people living in isolated villages, and it was not unusual for people to be attacked. Tigers have been known to enter houses and drag sleeping villagers from their beds. Although most tigers do not kill human beings, once a tiger has killed a person, they are more likely to do so again.

Language tip
Mnemonics are phrases that help us to remember tricky spellings. You can use ones other people have created, or come up with your own!

For example, to spell 'because', remember: **B**ig **E**lephants **C**an **A**lways **U**nderstand **S**maller **E**lephants

 Stretch zone

Make a list of things that could be done to help solve the conflicts between humans and animals in a humane way. Use ideas from the email plus ideas of your own.

The Man-eating Tiger

Mohsin was an old man. As a young man, he had been a soldier and he wanted his only son to have a career in the army. So, just after his eighteenth birthday, Mohsin's son Ali travelled to the town, some distance away. He was accepted into the
5   army and given two days' leave before starting his training.

When Ali arrived back in the village, a crowd of villagers welcomed him. They told him that his father was working on his land at the farthest end of the village and would not be back before nightfall. So, after lunch with his neighbours, a
10 party of about 20 young men set off to gather leaves for cattle fodder. For several months the villagers had gathered leaves only from nearby trees, because two women collecting grass had been killed by a tiger in the surrounding forest. But now there were not enough leaves to feed the cattle, and the men
15 had to go into the forest again. They walked beyond the cultivated fields, up the valley and into the dense forest.

Language tip
Determiners come before nouns and give us more information about nouns, such as articles ('a', 'an', 'the'), number/quantifier ('one', 'some'), possession ('my', 'your') and demonstratives ('this', 'those').

Find examples of some of these in this extract.

- Express opinions about a story

Here the men separated, each one climbing a tree and cutting the thin branches. They then tied them into bundles and returned as quickly as they could to the village. Each man sang as he
20 walked to keep up his courage. From among the trees, the man-eating tiger heard the men's voices. Silently, he left his cover and followed a cattle track across the stream.

Ali was high in a bauhinia tree, the upper branches of which leaned over a small ravine. The tiger saw Ali and hid himself
25 behind a fallen tree some distance away. Ali finished cutting the leaves and started to bundle them up. He noticed that two of the branches which he had cut had fallen into the ravine. He jumped down to collect them. As he bent to pick up the branches, the tiger leaped on him and killed him.

30 Mohsin returned to the village at sunset and was delighted to hear that his son had been accepted in the army. But why had Ali not returned from gathering fodder? Mohsin shut up his cattle safely for the night, and still his son had not returned. Darkness was falling and the villagers were inside their houses
35 for the night. Mohsin took a lantern and went out to look for Ali.

Glossary

bauhinia beautiful flowering tree, also known as an orchid tree, which grows in tropical countries
ravine narrow valley or gorge with steep sides

Like all the villagers, Mohsin knew that a man-eating tiger had killed there. Nevertheless, he spent the entire night crossing and re-crossing the forest as he searched for his son. As the
40 sun rose the next day, Mohsin was resting on a rock above the ravine when he saw blood glinting on a nearby stone. He knew then, even before he found Ali's body, that his son was dead.

Not long afterwards, the man-eating tiger was hunted and shot. Mohsin was satisfied.

Comprehension

A

1 Why did the young men go off to gather leaves in a large group?

2 What mistake did Ali make when gathering the leaves, which resulted in his death?

B

1 What effect does asking a question have in the story? (lines 31–32)

2 The last line says that Mohsin was satisfied when the tiger was killed. Describe what you think the writer meant by 'satisfied'.

C

1 Describe Mohsin's character. Do the same for Ali. Were they brave or foolish?

Write a story about an animal

You have read several stories about animals in this unit. Now it's your turn to write a story involving an animal. Your story may be true or imaginary. You may like to write about your pet, or a wild animal. Discuss your ideas and compare your planning with a partner.

- Identify some features you have found effective in the stories you have read.

- Think of an idea for a good plot for an animal story, perhaps involving someone in danger, a conflict between humans and animals, or an example of humans and animals helping one another.

- Plan your story carefully, including precise details about the setting and the human and animal characters. Describe the nature of the relationship and the dilemmas they face, and include a dramatic scene during your story.

- Use clues in a story to answer questions
- Give own opinions clearly and confidently
- Plan your story, proofread it and correct errors
- Think about sentence construction, punctuation and organizing your writing

?

Do you think the tiger should have been shot? Should we be more tolerant of wild animals? Can you think of any other solution to the villagers' problem?

Learning tip

If you are struggling to plan your story, you could use a story mountain to create a structure:

- **Opening** (we start our ascent)
- **Build-up** (we are moving towards the top of the mountain and tension is growing)
- **Climax** (we have made it to the top of the mountain and the big dilemma)
- **Resolution** (the characters are finding ways to resolve the dilemma)
- **Ending** (we have reached the foot of the mountain again and there is resolution to the story).

How do we manage scarce resources?

> **The perpetual struggle for room and food ...**
>
> *Essay on the Principle of Population,*
> THOMAS MALTHUS

Talk about ...

- Find out how much the population in your country has increased in the past 200 years.
- What problems might be caused by an increase in population?

Some experts now think that by 2030 there will be 8.5 billion people on Earth. There are many problems caused by this growing population. Our Earth has a great many valuable resources, such as water, minerals, and fertile, productive land. This unit will look at steps we can take to make sure there is enough of all these to go around.

• Contribute to discussions and share own ideas

Can we create more land for people to live on?

The Netherlands means 'the low-lying lands', and it is one of the world's most densely populated countries. There are 485 people per square kilometre, and one quarter of the country is below sea level.

The Dutch have been reclaiming land from the sea for centuries. In fact, a thousand years ago, 60 per cent of the Netherlands was underwater.

Look at the two maps of the Netherlands below. Can you tell what percentage of the land has been reclaimed from the sea?

Talk about ...

• What do you know about the Netherlands?

• Can you find the Netherlands on a European map?

• What sort of natural features can you find in the Netherlands?

The parts of the Netherlands, in north western Europe, which are above sea level

The parts of the Netherlands, which are reclaimed land (areas in white)

Word origins

nether (adj), an old English word, meaning 'low'. It gives the Netherlands and the lower part of the River Rhine that flows through Germany its name: *Neder Rijn* in Dutch.

- Contribute to discussions and share own ideas

Can we build artificial islands?

This is Palm Jumeirah Island in Dubai (the photograph on the left, below). It is a man-made island built for tourists in the shallow waters of the Arabian Gulf, where the waves are no more than two metres high.

Designed by a Dutch construction company with experience in land reclamation, it also inspired the proposed design of a new island off the coast of the Netherlands some years ago. This island was never built.

The plan was for an island 50 kilometres long that would have provided extra land for housing and farming. "We are hungry for land," said a Dutch politician. "We need a huge area for building." As in other countries, the population of the Netherlands is expanding.

If it had been built, this island would have been in the stormy North Sea, where waves can be ten metres high. Scientists agree that sea levels are likely to rise in the future. This means that the island would have had to have been built high above sea level, which would have been very expensive.

Environmentalists opposed the plan. Building the island would have required hundreds of millions of tonnes of sand and sea to be moved. They were worried about the effect this would have had on the marine life in the area. The real effects of building the island would not have been known until after it had been built.

Talk about ...

Do you think islands should be created? With a partner, make a list of reasons for and against building artificial islands.

Marker Wadden, an artificial archipelago which has been successfully created in Lake Markermeer, Netherlands. Rather than solving a housing shortage for people, these islands have been created to provide a wetland habitat for wildlife.

Palm Jumeirah Island, Dubai

Presenting your design for an island

Imagine that you have been asked to enter a competition to design a new island. You are one of ten designers and at the end of the competition, one design will be chosen.

When you draw an image of your island, will you look at digital maps on the internet, photographs of real islands, or some of the fantastic images from the early days of exploration? Think about the people who will settle there, and what kind of life they will lead.

- Create a drawing of your proposed island and give it a name.
- Decide where in the world this island should be.
- What would your island be used for?
- Write a short presentation, arguing the case for why your island should be built.

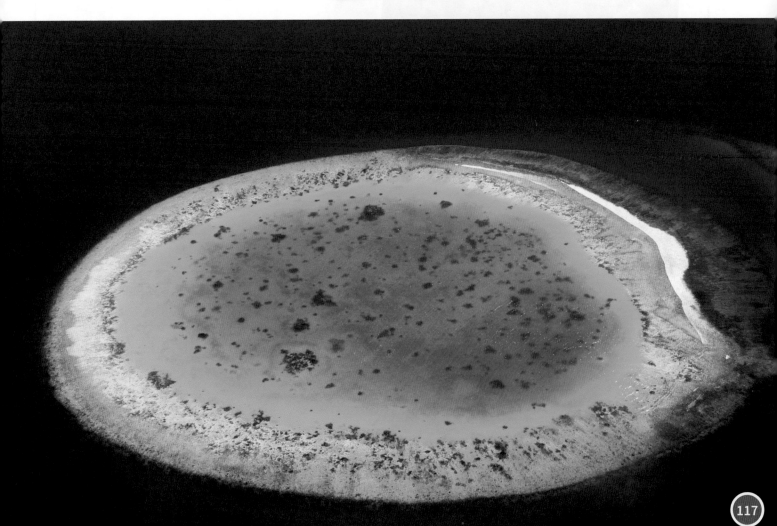

Writing and punctuating speech

Look at the characters and the information provided about them on these two pages.

- Talk about the lives of the characters.
- Imagine what the characters may be thinking and feeling in their situation.
- Think of appropriate comments for each of the speech bubbles.
- Use the sort of language each character in the picture would use.
- Write out what each person might be saying, using direct speech.

> - Use a suitable style of English for the purpose of writing

Adanna's house is very close to an airport. The aircraft fly low over her house and it is very noisy.

Saad lives near a golf course. The golf course requires a lot of water for maintenance, but this is water he and other local people need.

Fergus is a tourist who plays golf at the golf course near to Saad's home.

- Use a suitable style of English for the purpose of writing
- Use correct punctuation for direct speech

Tamanda's village is in an area where the land is over-grazed and there is no longer enough food for the community's animals.

Language tip
When you punctuate **direct speech**, you need to show who is speaking, and what they are saying. It also helps to use **descriptive verbs** that reflect the attitude of the speaker.
For example: "I'm going to be late again," sighed the businessman.

João is a fisherman. Over-fishing has reduced the number of fish in the sea near where he lives.

Yukio works in an office in a big city. Many commuters drive to work in the city every day and it creates one big traffic jam.

How do we share resources fairly?

Problems can be overcome by dividing resources more equally. The following text is a folk tale from Ethiopia. It is about two brothers whose rich old father died, and left all his wealth and land to his proud and selfish elder son. His younger son, who was kind, considerate and goodhearted, only received a rooster with fine red feathers.

The Red Rooster

Harvest time came, and the elder brother gathered in his crops and filled his grain stores until they were overflowing, but he never gave any grain to the younger man.

"It can't be helped," the younger brother said to his wife. "No
5 doubt he needs all the grain for himself."

The rich brother sometimes gave feasts for his friends, but he never invited his brother.

"Ah well," the younger brother said. "He is still my brother, after all." Then, one day, the elder brother fell ill. He sent for
10 the medicine man who came to examine him.

"You won't get better," the medicine man said, "unless you eat the flesh of a big rooster with fine red feathers."

"I haven't got a rooster," the sick man cried.

"No, but your brother has," said his wife. "That horrid thing!
15 It wakes me up every morning with its ugly crowing."

"Then go and ask my brother to give it to me," the older brother moaned. "And hurry up. I feel so ill I'm sure I'm about to die."

His wife ran to the younger brother's house.

"Your elder brother's ill," she said. "And the only thing that
20 can cure him is the flesh of a big rooster with fine red feathers."

"Husband," said the younger brother's wife. "That rooster is the only thing we have."

Her husband frowned at her.

"If my brother needs it, he must have it," he said.

Language tip

A **modal verb** is usually used when something hasn't happened yet. It is used with another verb to express ability ('can/can't'), permission ('may'), possibility ('could') or obligation ('ought to').

Examples from 'The Red Rooster': 'can't', 'won't' and 'will'.

Glossary

medicine man person in charge of a tribe's health, using traditional remedies to cure illnesses

25 So he gave the rooster to his brother's wife, and she took it away and killed it and gave its meat to the sick man to eat.

Very soon the elder brother began to feel better.

"Slaughter one of our animals," he said to his wife. "Make a feast. Invite my friends. Let's celebrate my recovery."

30 But he didn't invite his brother.

The feast was at its height and everyone was sitting at their ease, enjoying the tasty stews, when the elder brother felt that something strange was happening to him. He touched his legs and felt his arms.

35 "Help!" he shouted. "What's happening to me? I'm growing feathers!"

His wife and all his guests jumped up in horror. It was true. Bright red feathers were growing all over the body of their host. The medicine man and the elders came running as soon

40 as they heard the news. They sat down together to discuss the problem.

"You've been greedy," they said at last to the sick man. "You took everything that your father left you and gave nothing to your brother. You even took his rooster, his only possession,

45 without a word of thanks, although he gave it to you freely and generously. You will be cursed and your feathers will grow until he has forgiven you."

At once the elder brother went to the younger brother and begged his forgiveness.

50 "Brother, forgive me," he said. "I've been selfish and greedy, and I took all you had without a word of thanks."

His younger brother embraced him affectionately.

"Of course I forgive you," he said, "for we are brothers, after all." At once the feathers dropped off the elder

55 brother and he had a man's skin again. He shared his property equally with his younger brother, and from that time on they lived in harmony with each other.

> **Language tip**
> **Imperative verbs** command someone to do something rather than request it. For example: "Slaughter one of our animals". (line 28)

121

- Use knowledge of language and structure when writing
- Vary the sentences you write by including different types of conjunctions
- Use a model text to help with own writing

Comprehension

1 What lesson do you think this folk tale teaches?
2 Why do you think the father left all of his property to the elder son?

1 What features of a folk tale can you find in this story?
2 Find a quotation from the text that shows that the younger brother is a much more caring person than anyone else in the story.
3 Find suitable alternatives for the verb 'said' in lines 4, 14, 19, 28, 42 and 53.

1 What would you have done in the younger brother's place?

 Stretch zone

List any words that are unfamiliar in the extract and look these up in a dictionary.

Now it's your turn to write a folk tale

Folk tales, like this one, are often simply written and constructed. They are usually designed to illustrate some kind of message, often feature someone who is worthy, and include a moral or lesson. They usually reflect the culture and traditions of the area they come from.

- Write your own folk tale. It can relate to a story you know, or you can make it up entirely.
- Base your story around a message about the way people behave, or the problems they face.
- Use a simple, clear style, and use paragraphs to structure your story. Remember to include different types of sentences.

Learning tip
When you are planning a story, try not to squeeze in too many characters or dramatic events. Think about your reader and try to ensure they will be able to follow what is happening and will be excited to find out what happens next.

An illustration of a traditional folk tale from East Asia

• Identify the theme of a poem

What's the theme of this poem?

Countries can be greedy as well as individuals. Which countries do you think use up most of the Earth's resources, and which use the least?

John Agard was born in Guyana and came to Britain as an adult in 1977. He was thinking about questions like this when he wrote the poem below.

?

How could the Earth's resources be more evenly distributed? Do you think we will ever be able to make the distribution truly equal? Why? Why not?

I'd like to squeeze

I'd like to squeeze this round world
        into a new shape

    I'd like to squeeze this round world
        like a tube of toothpaste

    I'd like to squeeze this round world
        fair and square

    I'd like to squeeze it and squeeze it
        till everybody had an equal share

JOHN AGARD

- Identify and discuss ideas in poems
- Write different types of poems
- Use literary devices to make writing interesting

Comprehension

A

1 Explain how John Agard thinks that 'squeezing' would help the world.

2 What do you think the writer wants everybody to have an equal share of?

B

1 'Like a tube of toothpaste' is a simile. Think of some more similes which would fit this line.

2 There is no punctuation in this poem. Why do you think the writer chose to use none?

3 Which words are repeated in the poem? What effect does the repetition have?

C

1 Why do you think the writer has set out his poem in this shape?

Now create your own shape poem

John Agard's poem is very simple. He uses shape and repetition to put across his ideas.

- Write your own poem about the world's limited resources, in the style of Agard's poem.
- Think of a picture in your head to develop in your poem.

A story about survival on an island

Robinson Crusoe is a novel by Daniel Defoe that was published over 300 years ago in 1719.

After he was shipwrecked on a tropical island, a long way from civilization, Crusoe managed to survive with only a few objects saved from the ship, including a gun and a packet of barley seeds. This short extract is about his struggle to produce the first crop in his new island home.

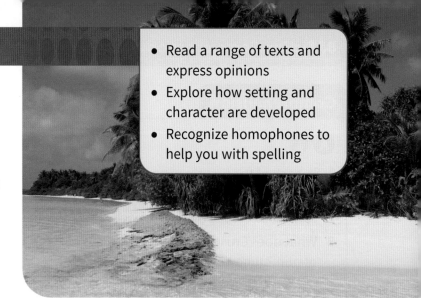

- Read a range of texts and express opinions
- Explore how setting and character are developed
- Recognize homophones to help you with spelling

My first harvest

The ground I had dug up for my crop of barley was not large, for I only had a small amount of seed. My hopes of gathering seed from my first crop had been destroyed. I had planted my first crop in the dry season and it had failed. I was pleased to
5   see my new crop growing well, but then I saw that I was in danger of losing it. Wild goats were devouring it. They were eating the green shoots as soon as they pushed through the earth.

With a great deal of hard work I made a hedge to fence in my crop and tied my dog to the little gate which I also made. He
10 barked all night long, the wild goats kept away and my barley grew strong and green. As it began to ripen and form ears of seed, my hopes of being able to make bread also grew.

But then my crop was under threat of ruin once more when I found flocks of fowl pecking at the seeds. I immediately shot
15 at them, for I always had my gun with me, but more birds returned. I realized that they would destroy all my hopes and I would starve. I examined the damage and found that if I could save what was left of my crop all was not lost.

I killed three of the birds and hung their bodies from the
20 trees. The effect was marvellous. So long as my scarecrows hung there, the fowls came neither to my crops again, nor even to my part of the island. This I was very glad of, and at about the end of December, I harvested my crop. I was very relieved, and I now believed I would
25 be able to supply myself with bread.

From *Robinson Crusoe* by DANIEL DEFOE

> **Language tip**
> **Homophones** are words that sound the same or almost the same, but have a different spelling and meaning. Find homophones for 'maid', 'moor', 'foul' and 'affect' in this extract.

- Discuss the context and setting of a story
- Write from a character's point of view
- Recognize homophones to help you with spelling

Comprehension

1 In each of the first three paragraphs, Crusoe talks about his 'hopes'. Explain what his hopes are.

2 How does Crusoe overcome each of the problems he faces?

3 What does Crusoe mean when he says his crop is 'under threat of ruin'? (line 13)

1 Look at the way 'there' and 'their' are used in paragraph 4. These words are homophones, words that are pronounced the same, but are spelled differently and have different meanings. Explain the meanings of 'there' and 'their' in this text.

1 Crusoe was stranded on his island more than 300 years ago. Give some reasons why this would be less likely to happen today.

Talk about ...
Discuss with a partner how you think Crusoe must have felt when he realized he was likely to be on the island for a long time.

Writing from the goats' point of view

Robinson Crusoe had to defend his crop of barley from the wild goats and the birds. Write an account in the form of a journal written from the goats' point of view. What is their side of the story?

Saving the life of a friend

This story is set in Andalucía, Spain, in 1936. Antonito lives on his parents' bull farm where he rides his horse, Chica, and looks after a little bull calf called Paco. Life is good until he discovers that Paco is going to be sent to the bullring when he is big enough. Antonito knows well that the end of the fight with a matador always ends in the bull's death. Antonito cannot bear to think that his beloved Paco will die that way, and he plans to run away from his parents' farm, and take Paco with him. But in 1936, a civil war was being fought in Spain, and Antonito does not realize the danger he and his family are in.

Glossary

toro bull used in Spanish bullfighting

matador bullfighter

corral enclosure or pen for horses, cattle, and other animals

corrida Spanish word for bullfight

herd group of animals that stick together for protection and to form a community

droning constant, repeated sound, like the buzzing of bees, or the sound of a (distant) aeroplane

Toro! Toro!

That same night I lay in my bed forcing myself to stay awake. I waited until the house fell silent about me, until I was as sure as I could be that everyone was asleep. The sound of Father's deep snoring was enough to convince me that it was safe
5   to move.

I was already dressed under my blankets. I stole out of the house and across the moonlit yard towards the stable. The dogs whined at me, but I patted them and they did not bark. I led Chica out of her stable, mounting her some way down
10   the farm track, out of sight of the house, and then rode out over the farm towards Paco's corral.

My idea was clumsy but simple. I knew that to separate Paco from the others, to release him on his own would be almost impossible, and that even if I succeeded, sooner or later he
15   would be bound to come running back to the others. He was after all a herd animal. I would have to release them all, all of them together, and drive them as far as I could up into the cork forests where they could lose themselves and never be found. Even if they caught a few of them, Paco might be lucky. At
20   least this way he stood some chance of avoiding the horrors of the *corrida*.

The cattle shifted in the corral as I came closer. They were nervous, unsettled by this strange night-time visitor. I dismounted at the gate and opened it. For some while they stood looking
25   at me, snorting, shaking their horns. I called out quietly into the night. "Paco! Paco! It's me. It's Antonito!"

I knew he would come, and he did, walking slowly towards me, his ears twitching and listening all the time as I sweetened him closer. Then, as he reached the open gate, the others began
30 to follow him. It all happened so fast after that. To begin with, they came at a gentle walk through the gate. Then they were trotting, then jostling, then galloping, charging past me. Paco, I felt sure, was gone with them, swept along in the stampede.

I don't know what it was that knocked me senseless, only that
35 when I woke, I was not alone. Paco was standing over me, looking down at me, and Chica was grazing nearby. Whether Paco had saved me from being trampled to death, I do not know. What I did know was that my plan had worked perfectly, better than I could ever have hoped for.

40 I got to my feet slowly, amazed that nothing was broken. I was not badly hurt at all, just a little bruised, and my cheek was cut. [...]

I had in mind to go as far as I could, as fast as I could, before dawn. Beyond that I had no thought as to where we would go,
45 nor what I would do with him. As we climbed the rutty tracks up into the hills, I felt inside me a sudden surge of elation. Paco was free and now I would keep him free. I had no conscience any more about what I had done, no thought now of what it would mean to Father to lose his precious herd of cattle. Paco
50 would not suffer that terrible death in the ring – that was all that mattered to me. I had done it, and I was ecstatic.

Chica seemed to know the path, and she was as surefooted as a mule. I never once came near to falling off, despite my exhaustion. Behind us, Paco was finding it more difficult, but
55 he was managing. [...]

We came suddenly into a clearing. On the far side was a stone hut, most of it in ruins, and beside it a circular stone corral. I hadn't seen this one before, but I had seen others. There were several like it scattered through the cork forests, built for
60 gathering cattle or sheep or goats. Paco followed us in and I shut the gate behind him. Both Paco and Chica at once began nuzzling the grass. I lay down in the shelter of the wall, and was asleep before I knew it.

Cork oak forest

128

- Read and compare stories
- Contribute to discussions and share own ideas

The warming sun woke me, that or the cry of the vultures.
65 They were circling above us in the blue. The mist had all gone.
Paco lay beside me, chewing the cud and licking his nose. Chica
stood, resting her fourth leg, only half awake. I lay there for a
while, trying to gather my thoughts.

That was when I heard the sound of distant droning, like a
70 million bees. There were no bees to be seen, and nothing else
either. I thought I must be imagining things, but then Paco was
on his feet and snorting. The vultures were suddenly gone.
The droning was coming closer, ever closer, until it became a
throbbing angry roar that filled the air about us. Then I saw
75 them, flying low over the ridge towards us, dozens of them:
airplanes with black crosses on their wings. They came right
over us, their engines thunderous, throbbing so loudly that it
hurt my ears.

In my terror I curled up against the wall and covered my ears.
80 Paco was going wild and Chica, too, was circling the corral,
looking for a way out. I waited until the planes were gone,
then climbed up on to the wall of the corral. They were diving
now, their engines screaming, diving on Sauceda, diving on
my home.

85 I saw the smoke of the first bombs before I heard the distant
crunch of the explosions. It was as if some vengeful thing was
pounding the village with his fist, each punch sending up a
plume of fire, until the whole village was covered in a pall
of smoke.

90 I stood there on the corral wall, trying not to believe what my
eyes were telling me. They were telling me that my whole world
was being destroyed, that Father and Mother and Maria were
down there somewhere in that smoke and fire. I don't think I
really believed it until the planes had gone, until I heard the
95 sound of silence again, and then the sound of my own crying.

From *Toro! Toro!* by MICHAEL MORPURGO

Comprehension

A

1 Why is Antonito running away?
2 What does he plan to do to save Paco?
3 What happens to Antonito's village?

B

1 What do you think the writer means by 'I sweetened him closer'? (lines 28–29)
2 What symbolic role do you think the vultures play?

C

1 Do you think that bullfighting is a cruel sport?
2 Do you think Antonito was justified in his actions?
3 Think back to Unit 7 and everything you have read in this unit. Do you think humans and animals live well and fairly together?

Stretch zone

Note any words that are unfamiliar in the extract and look up their meaning in a dictionary.

How do we see others and ourselves?

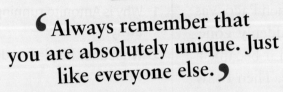

'Always remember that you are absolutely unique. Just like everyone else.'

MARGARET MEAD

Talk about ...

- Who are you? What makes you stand out from others in your family or in your class?
- Think of all the people around the world. Think of your family and friends. What is similar or different about them?

Margaret Mead, the American author and anthropologist, believed that we are who we are because of our cultural upbringing, and this is what causes our similarities and differences. With all the different cultures in the world, it's not surprising that people are so different, but we are also similar in many ways. By drawing attention to the fact that we are 'more alike' than 'unalike', we can support the idea that we should live together in harmony, despite our differences.

Word origins

identity (n), from the Latin word *idem*, meaning 'same'
Related words:
- identical
- identify
- identification

Writing a self-description

Make a list of the things that make you the same as other people and the things that make you different to others.

- Contribute to discussions and share own ideas
- Use knowledge of language and text structure when writing
- Understand how the structure of a story can fit its purpose

Learning tip

When comparing similarities and differences between two things, it can be useful to use a T chart, with one column entitled 'Similarities', and the other column entitled 'Differences'.

What do fables tell us about identity?

A fable is a simple story which can be understood on a metaphorical level. It is a story with a moral. This means that it has a message in it that will teach you something about human behaviour. Many fables are about animals, but the moral is about human behaviour. Fables often include ideas about people's identity as individuals and as communities. Read the two fables on the following pages and think about their similarities and differences.

Stretch zone

Look at the word *metaphorical.* Write down what you think the definition for the word is, then check in a dictionary to see if you were correct.

The Obvious Elephant

One day long ago, the people
of a village woke to find a
huge, grey animal in the
middle of their field. No
5   one knew what it was
or how it had got there.
The children ran round
it excitedly, and
prodded it with sticks.
10   One of them poked it
in the eye. The grown-
ups laughed as they,
too, prodded the poor
animal. Some villagers
15   were afraid of the strange
monster and went back
indoors. Someone threw a
stone. At that moment,
the Professor came along.

20   "Stop all this immediately!" he ordered.
"I will find out what this animal is."

The Professor went to his library and found out.

"It's an ELEPHANT!" he told the villagers.

"Oh! That's what it is! It's an ELEPHANT!" cried
25   the villagers.

And when they knew what he was, they made him welcome.
They made him a necklace of flowers for his huge neck and
gave him a name. From then on the villagers looked after the
elephant and they lived together happily ever after.

Retold from *The Obvious Elephant* by Bruce Robinson

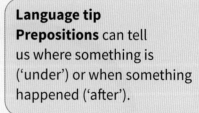

Language tip
Prepositions can tell
us where something is
('under') or when something
happened ('after').

132

- Read and compare fables
- Contribute to discussions and share own ideas

A fable by Aesop

There was once a man and a lion who were travelling together on a long journey. As they walked along, they talked about many things. The lion boasted that he was stronger and braver than a man, and the man boasted that he was stronger and
5 braver than a lion.

"Of course, a man is stronger than a lion," boasted the man. "Think of all the battles they have won!"

"Of course, a lion is stronger than a man," boasted the lion, "Think how much bigger the lion is!"

10 As they continued to argue, they came to a crossroads where there was a statue of a man strangling a lion.

"There you are!" cried the man. "Is that not proof that a man is stronger than a lion?"

"Wait a moment, wait a moment," said the lion. "That is just
15 your view. If we lions could make statues, I am sure we would see the lion winning the fight!"

Comprehension

 A

1 What similarities are there between the two fables?
2 What differences between them can you find?

 B

1 Why is 'ELEPHANT' written in upper case letters in 'The Obvious Elephant'?
2 Why is the phrase 'Wait a moment' repeated in the fable by Aesop?

 C

1 What lesson is the fable about the elephant teaching us?
2 What is the lesson being taught in the fable by Aesop?

- Write a fable
- Use a model text to help with own writing
- Use knowledge of language and text structure when writing

Write your own fable

Now it is your turn to write a fable. Your discussion should have given you some ideas for a message or moral for a fable.

- Think of the moral you would like to write about.
- Think of an appropriate setting. Keep your story simple.
- Decide on your characters. What kinds of people and animals will feature in your fable?
- Include the structure and language used in fables you have seen and read.

What is the identity of a community?

For many people, their identity is strongly bound up with their country or where they live. This means that feeling a part of their country or community is very important to them.

A story about a country girl in the city

The following extract is set in the 1820s, in Switzerland and Germany. Heidi, an orphan, was sent to live with her grandfather in the Swiss mountains. However, as she was not attending school, she has been taken to live with a family in Frankfurt by her Aunt Dete to be a companion for Klara, a girl whose ill health means she cannot walk. Klara has a strict governess called Fraulein Rottenmeier. While Heidi likes Klara, she cannot help longing for the mountains and her friends and family there, including a special goat named Snowflake.

Glossary

Frankfurt city in Germany
Fraulein German for 'Miss'; an unmarried woman
governess woman employed to teach children in a private home

Still from the 2015 film *Heidi*, showing Heidi's new life in Frankfurt

- Read a range of texts and express opinions

Missing the mountains

Klara had grown much more cheerful; she no longer found time hang heavy during the lesson hours, for Heidi was continually making a diversion of some kind or other. She jumbled all her letters up together and seemed quite unable to learn them, and
5 when the tutor tried to draw her attention to their different shapes, and to help her by showing her that this was like a little horn, or that like a bird's bill, she would suddenly exclaim in a joyful voice, "That is a goat!" "That is a bird of prey!" For the tutor's descriptions suggested all kinds of pictures to her
10 mind, but left her still incapable of the alphabet. In the later afternoons Heidi always sat with Klara, and then she would give the latter many and long descriptions of the mountain and of her life upon it, and the burning longing to return would become so overpowering that she always finished with the
15 words, "Now I must go home! To-morrow I must really go!"

After dinner Heidi had to sit alone in her room for a couple of hours, for she understood now that she might not run about outside at Frankfurt as
20 she did on the mountain, and so she did not attempt it. So Heidi had plenty of time from day to day to sit and picture how everything at home was now turning green, and how the yellow
25 flowers were shining in the sun, and how all around lay bright in the warm sunshine, the snow and the rocks, and the whole wide valley, and Heidi at times could hardly contain herself for
30 the longing to be back home again. And Dete had told her that she could go home whenever she liked.

So it came about one day that Heidi felt she could not bear it any longer, and in haste she put on her straw hat, and went
35 downstairs. But just as she reached the hall-door she met Fraulein Rottenmeier herself, just returning from a walk, which put a stop to Heidi's journey.

- Use clues in a text to answer questions
- Discuss the context and setting of a story

Fraulein Rottenmeier stood still a moment, looking at her from top to toe in blank astonishment. Then she broke out,—

40 "What have you dressed yourself like that for? What do you mean by this? Have I not strictly forbidden you to go running about in the streets?"

"I was not going to run about, I was going home," said Heidi, frightened.

45 Then Heidi's feelings got the better of her, and she poured forth her trouble. "Indeed I only want to go home, for if I stay so long away Snowflake will begin crying again, and grandmother is waiting for me, and I can never see how the sun says good-night to the mountains; and if the great bird were to fly over
50 Frankfurt he would croak louder than ever about people huddling all together and teaching each other bad things, and not going to live up on the rocks, where it is so much better."

From *Heidi* by Johanna Spyri, translated from German by Mabel Abbott

Glossary

croak say in a deep, harsh voice

huddle crowd together

Comprehension

1 What had made Klara more cheerful?
2 Why was Heidi desperate to get back to the mountains?
3 What things did Heidi do each day?

1 What does 'time hang heavy' mean? (line 2)
2 Find an example of anthropomorphism, where human actions are given to non-human objects, in the extract.
3 What words would you use to describe Heidi's character?

1 What do you think of the tutor's method of teaching Heidi the alphabet?
2 Later, Heidi is able to show Klara the mountains she has described to her. Do you think sharing this experience might strengthen their friendship? Give reasons for your answer.

Talk about ...

- Do you think the mountains are an important part of Heidi's identity?
- Is she the same person in Frankfurt as she is in the mountains with her family and Snowflake?
- Is where you live an important part of your identity? Why? Why not?

- Read a non-fiction text and discuss its features

What does it mean to have more than one identity?

As you saw in Unit 4, people's sense of their own identity can be complicated if they or their families have moved to different countries. It can be difficult living in a country with different traditions and beliefs to the ones you have grown up with.

Naomi Shihab Nye is an Arab-American poet. She was born in America, but you can see from what she writes about herself that her family still identifies closely with the Middle East.

A flavour of the Middle East

All my life I thought about the Middle East, wrote about it, wondered about it, lived in it, visited it, worried about it, loved it. We are blessed and doomed at
5 the same time.

I was born in the United States, but my father stared back toward the Middle East whenever he stood outside. Our kitchen smelled like
10 the Middle East – garlic and pine nuts sizzled in olive oil, fried eggplant, hot pita bread. My father dropped sprigs of mint into our pots of hot tea. He had been happy
15 as a boy in the Old City of Jerusalem with his Palestinian and Greek and Jewish and Armenian neighbors. But after the sad days of 1948, when his family lost their home and everything they
20 owned, he wanted to go away. He was one of the few foreign university students in Kansas in the 1950s, and was a regular customer at the local drugstore soda fountain in his new little town.

"He always looked dreamy, preoccupied, like he could see
25 things other people couldn't see," the druggist told me twenty-five years later. Well yes, I thought. That's what immigrants look like. They always have other worlds in their minds.

Aubergine fatteh

Glossary

eggplant American English for 'aubergine'

pita bread, also spelled 'pitta', flat bread traditional in Middle Eastern and Mediterranean cuisine

soda fountain machine that dispenses soft drinks

- Use clues in a text to answer questions
- Use patterns and rules to help you to spell words correctly
- Use the internet to check spellings

My father and my American mother invented new dishes using Middle Eastern ingredients. We were proud without knowing

30 it. Travelers from the Middle East often sat in circles in our backyard sharing figs and peaches and speaking in Arabic. Arabic music played in our house. Our father told better folk stories than anyone else's father – he had a gentle wit

35 and almost never got mad. So kids from the neighborhood would camp out on our screened-in back porch, and we would all beg my father

40 to tell more funny stories. It was a rich world to be in.

From the introduction to *19 Varieties of Gazelle: Poems of the Middle East* by NAOMI SHIHAB NYE

Comprehension

1 Did the writer's father go to live in the US as a teenager or an adult? Give evidence from the text to support your answer.

2 Do you think the writer's father was a sociable man? Give evidence from the text to support your answer.

1 The writer mentions the 'drugstore'. What word would British English use for this American English word?

2 Because the writer has been brought up in America, she uses American spelling and expressions. In British English, 'neighbour' has a 'u'. Can you find any other American English spellings and words in the text?

1 Can you think of any other examples of American English spellings or words that people use today? You could use the internet to do some research.

2 In lines 40–41, the writer says 'It was a rich world to be in'. What makes a 'rich world', in your opinion?

Stretch zone

With a partner, discuss the ways in which the writer and her family keep the Middle East in their lives even though they are living in America.

Writing memories

Now try writing about your own memories of moving from one place to another, or imagine that you are moving somewhere entirely new. You could write about a place that at first seemed quite strange and that has since become familiar to you.

- Is there somewhere that you would like to go back to?
- The first person 'I' may be you, a member of your family or a character you have made up. The memories may be real or imagined.
- Use the past tense. Plan what to put in each of your paragraphs and think of an interesting way to conclude your composition.

- Write grammatically correct sentences
- Be adventurous with sentences and language to create an effect
- Use suitable vocabulary for the topic

Learning tip

Look back at other units in this course you are familiar with. Make a note of the different types of fiction texts you have looked at. In small groups, list the features of each type of text. You can refer to the list as you plan and write your own fiction texts.

Our parents told us that we would be going to live in the United Kingdom. We felt a bit scared but also excited at the idea.

An interview with an actor

This is an interview with AJ, an actor who performs on stage and on television. What is it like to become someone else as your job?

- Talk about the differences between written and spoken language
- Do research and prepare for an interview

Meet AJ: an up-and-coming star

Interviewer: Hi, AJ. Thanks for saying you'll answer a few questions. What made you want to become an actor?

AJ: Oh wow! Well, when I was younger, I fancied the fame and money. I wasn't very academic! I was also big into movies and liked to copy the characters who were in my favourite films.

Interviewer: What do you like most about being an actor?

AJ: I like looking through the eyes of someone else and walking in their shoes. Also, it's great to act badly and have no repercussions! I also like to collaborate with people who aren't actors and have other creative talents, like directors.

Interviewer: How do you get into character?

AJ: Oh, that's a big topic! You normally start by thinking about what happened to the person before the film or play begins: where they were born, what they were like in school, their background, their body language; a lot of it's to do with how this person would react in the situation shown in the film.

Interviewer: Do your fans ever think you're actually the character you play rather than an actor?

AJ: Yeah, all the time, and many people will sort of shout out your character's name when you walk down the street. They're surprised when you're not like that character in real life.

Glossary

act means both behave in a certain way and perform a part in a play or film

Now you're the interviewer

What famous character would you like to play in a film? It can be a real-life person or a made-up one. With a partner, write some interview questions to ask your partner's chosen character. Prepare your questions carefully so that you get good answers, not just 'yes' or 'no'. Make sure they are grammatically correct. Take turns role-playing the interviewer and the character being interviewed.

Learning tip

Closed questions invite very simple 'yes' or 'no' answers and are good for quick fact-finding.

For example: 'Are you busy?'

Open questions require a fuller, more interesting answer.

For example: 'How do you feel?'

A poem about belonging

Some people identify strongly with their country or community. What
happens if you feel that you do not belong to any country? This feeling
is what the following poem is about.

Citizen of the World

When you are very small
maybe not quite born
your parents move
for some reason you may never
5   understand they move
from their own town
from their own land
and you grow up in a place
that is never quite your home

10   and all your childhood people
with a smile or a fist say
you're not from here are you
and part of you says fiercely yes I am
and part of you feels no I'm not
15   I belong to where my parents belonged

but when you go to their town, their country
people there also say
you're not from here are you
and part of you says no I'm not
20   and part of you says fiercely yes I am
and so you grow up both and neither
and belong everywhere and nowhere much the same
both stronger and weaker for the lack of ground
able to fly but not to rest

25   and all over the world, though you feel alone
are millions like you, like a great flock of swallows
soaring or falling exhausted, wings beating the rhythm
of the wind that laughs at fences or frontiers,
whose home is itself, and the whole world it moves over.

DAVE CALDER

- Use clues in a poem to answer questions
- Use punctuation correctly
- Perform a poem

Comprehension

1 Why did the writer's parents move? Give some possible reasons why they left their home and their country to make a new life elsewhere.

2 What do you learn about the person whose point of view is given in the poem?

3 What do you think the title of the poem 'Citizen of the World' means?

1 What does 'with a smile or a fist' mean? (line 11)

2 Explain the comparison the writer makes between people and 'a great flock of swallows'. (lines 26–29)

3 How do the person's feelings change in the last stanza?

1 Have you ever felt like the person in the poem?

2 Do you think that the person will get over the problems that he/she faced early on?

Practise your punctuation

In poems, you are free to write without punctuation if you wish, just as Dave Calder does in most of his poem 'Citizen of the World'.

Practise writing sentences and punctuation by writing out the poem in continuous prose, adding capital letters and full stops.

Add any other punctuation marks, such as commas and parentheses, you think are necessary.

It's your turn to perform the poem!

This poem expresses strong feelings. You are going to prepare to perform the poem by colour-coding the different voices in it.

- On a copy of the poem, use three different colours to identify the different voices in it: the narrator, the other people, the young person.
- Choose how these different voices should be read out aloud in your class or group.
- Practise and then perform the poem. Think about how you can use your voices to enhance the reading.

• Do research for a short presentation

Why is language so important?

In Unit 4, you read about Amy Choi losing and then regaining the ability to speak Chinese. One of the important things which identifies you is the language you speak. Ralph Waldo Emerson (1803–82) was an American philosopher. He said: "Language is a city. Every human being brought a stone to the building of it." What do you think he meant by this?

Learn about minority languages

Do you know where each of the following six languages is spoken? In groups, find out a few facts about one of these languages to present to the rest of the class.

• Trumai
• Catawba
• Mavea
• Karaim
• Usku
• Bidyara

?

Imagine you speak a language at home that no one else you know speaks. Perhaps this is your reality and you do not have to imagine. How would you or do you feel about your home language?

These are just six of the world's 6,500 languages. These six languages are 'minority languages', which means that they are spoken by small numbers of people. Some minority languages have fewer than ten speakers left.

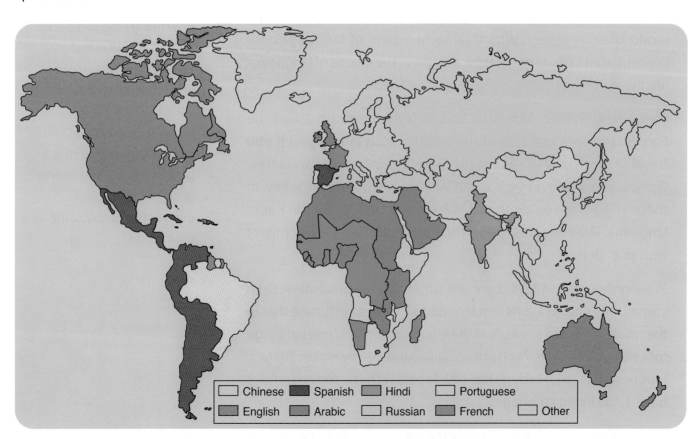

Chinese | Spanish | Hindi | Portuguese
English | Arabic | Russian | French | Other

A map showing the principal languages spoken in different areas of the world

The languages spoken in Papua New Guinea

Some researchers believe that half of the world's languages will have disappeared by the year 2100. Languages have been dying out throughout history. The difference now is that this is happening at an alarming rate. Why might this be?

- Read a variety of texts and consider their features
- Understand the difference between facts and opinions

Map showing Morobe province in Papua New Guinea

Vanishing languages

The deaths of languages are more noticeable in some parts of the world than in others. Where large numbers of languages are concentrated in small geographical regions, the deaths of languages are more obvious.

5   Papua New Guinea, Indonesia and Malaysia make up 2% of the Earth's land area but 25% of the world's living languages! If you travel to the tropical forests of the Morobe province in Papua New Guinea, you will find five isolated villages in a mountain valley. In these villages are fewer than 1,000 people who speak the Kapin
10   language. The villagers support themselves and have little contact with outsiders.

In neighbouring valleys there are other tiny communities. Each community speaks a different language. Linguists estimate that in the whole of Papua New Guinea there is approximately one language
15   for every 200 people. Papua New Guinea has 862 living languages; Indonesia has 701; Malaysia has 140. Together these three countries have 1,700 living languages!

The countries' isolation and mountain valleys are two reasons for the existence of so many languages. It is not surprising that as

Talk about ...

- How many languages are spoken in your class?
- Do all the languages use an alphabet like the one used in this book?
- How are they written? From left to right across a page? Or the opposite way?
- What makes them different to or the same as each other?

20   remote areas of the world have opened up for trade and tourism, more languages have died. Papua New Guinea has gold, silver and timber. These are valuable reserves, and people come to the islands to make money from them. With them come their own languages, and consequently more Papua New Guinea languages

25   will die and become extinct.

From *Vanishing Languages* by DAVID CRYSTAL

Schoolchildren in Papua New Guinea

Hold a group debate

Linguists believe that in one hundred years' time, half of the world's 6,500 living languages may be extinct. You may think it would be better if one language, a 'global language', was spoken by everyone all over the world. Or you may think that language is an important part of identity and all languages should be kept alive. Have a debate about these issues. The topic, or motion, is: 'We should have one global language'.

- Think of arguments for and against the statement you are debating.
- Discuss the issues in groups and decide whether your group will argue for or against the motion. Remember to listen carefully to others' opinions and add to your own list of arguments.
- During the debate, consider all arguments and explain your opinion.
- When you have finished your discussion, vote on the issue. Count how many of you are in favour of one global language, and how many think we should not have one, but many languages. What have you learned from the debate?

What happens to all our rubbish?

> ' One man's rubbish may be another's treasure '
>
> HECTOR URQUHART

Talk about ...

- What does the quotation mean?
- Have you ever used anything that someone else threw out? Toys? Clothes?
- The main image on this page shows a 'car boot sale' in the UK, where people sell their old possessions and other people buy them. Have you ever been to a similar kind of event?

When we throw rubbish into a bin, how often do we think about what will happen to it? Much of it is recycled, although the cost and energy required for recycling is often too high to ensure it gets done. A lot of rubbish goes to landfill sites and never decomposes, while other rubbish in these sites does decompose but produces dangerous gases, such as methane and carbon dioxide.

- Read a range of texts and express opinions

How can we reduce food waste?

According to the UN Environment Programme, every year around 30 per cent of food produced in the world is lost or wasted. This means that all the water, energy and time that went into producing the food is wasted, as well as the money which the production cost. It also means that decaying food, as well as perfectly good food, goes into landfill sites and can contribute to climate change by producing greenhouse gases. Organizations such as the UN Environment Programme are working on ways to tackle the problem of lost and wasted food.

Read the article below. In Bangkok, Thailand, well-known chefs and other food lovers from Thailand and Australia held an event where they prepared meals with ingredients that would have normally been thrown out in order to promote awareness of the 1.3 billion tonnes of food wasted each year.

Do you ever eat 'wonky' vegetables? They taste just the same, but are often wasted since we expect 'perfect' vegetables to be on sale in the supermarket.

Celebrity chefs serve up free meals from discarded food

For those who have never tried 'rejected' veggie curry made with 'saved' coconut milk served with 'broken rice' and washed down with corn cob tea, two United Nations agencies
5 have joined up with an Australian food charity for an event with a menu that also included 'fish scrap cake' and 'rescued' mango relish, accompanied by 'leftover' nine-grain followed by 'rescued' bread pudding for dessert.

10 If you were in Bangkok, Thailand, this week, those were some of the dishes prominent chefs and other food lovers from Thailand and Australia were preparing with ingredients that are usually discarded, to promote awareness
15 of 1.3 billion tonnes of food wasted each year.

The Think.Eat.Save event was organized by the UN Environment Programme (UNEP), the UN Food and Agricultural Organization (FAO) and the Australian food charity OzHarvest in
20 support of the new UN Sustainable Development Goals target to halve global food waste along production and supply chains by 2030.

Modelled on OzHarvest's annual Think.Eat. Save events, which feed thousands of people
25 across Australia, the Bangkok event had celebrity

chefs like Duangporn 'Bo' Songvisava, Dylan 'Lan' Jones, Chris Miller and Australian OzHarvest 'Chef for a Cause', Travis Harvey, who in May
30 this year opened Australia's first-ever food waste pop-up café, design a lunch menu using surplus produce saved from landfill or sourced from local farmers and suppliers.

The event is part of the Think.Eat.Save campaign
35 which was launched by the UNEP, the Food and Agricultural Organization and partners in 2013 to change the culture of food waste which results in 1.3 billion tonnes of food wasted globally each year, contributing to
40 greenhouse gas emissions. The total carbon footprint of food produced but not eaten is 3.3 Gt of carbon dioxide equivalent.

An estimated 20 to 40 per cent of food is lost or wasted along the supply chain in Asia Pacific
45 because food is lost in transit between rural production areas and urban consumers, and because of poor quality roads, hot and humid weather conditions, and poor packaging, according to UNEP.

From UN NEWS, December 2015

- Give your own opinions clearly and confidently
- Ask questions about others' views

Comprehension

 A

1 How many people in Australia benefit from OzHarvest's *Think. Eat. Save* events?

2 How does the 1.3 billion tonnes of food wasted harm the planet?

 B

1 Why do you think words such as 'rejected', 'saved' and 'rescued' are used to describe the food instead of 'food waste'?

2 What features of news reports are found in this news article?

 C

1 What could be done to reduce food waste in the supply chain between the areas of food production and where the food is consumed?

2 How do you think celebrity chefs can help the campaign to reduce food waste?

Talk about ...

Why is food wasted by:
- supermarkets?
- restaurants?
- households?

Stretch zone

Create a flyer encouraging families to reduce rubbish.

- Think about how you will grab people's attention.
- What facts will you include?
- Include eye-catching illustrations.

Present your research findings

Which group do you think can do the most to reduce food waste?

- Supermarkets
- Food banks
- Restaurants
- Children
- Parents
- Governments

Choose one of these groups and carry out research into how they could create policies, projects and events that reduce food waste and encourage people at home to do the same. You might take inspiration from the OzHarvest event you have read about, or come up with something entirely different.

Prepare a presentation to give to the rest of the class.

Trash or treasure?

Trash is the story of three boys, Raphael, Gardo and Rat, who live and work on the trash heaps of Behala, a fictional location loosely based on a place the author visited in the Philippines. They look for anything they can sell to earn money to survive. It is Raphael who tells the story.

Trash boy

I was a trash boy since I was old enough to move without help and pick things up. That was what? – three years old, and I was sorting.

Let me tell you what we're looking for.

5 Plastic, because plastic can be turned into cash, fast – by the kilo. White plastic is best, and that goes in one pile; blue in the next.

Paper, if it's white and clean – that means if we can clean it and dry it. Cardboard also.

10 Tin cans – anything metal. Glass, if it's a bottle. Cloth or rags of any kind – that means the occasional T-shirt, a pair of pants, a bit of sack that wrapped something up. The kids round here, half the stuff we wear is what we found, but most we pile up, weigh and sell. You should see me, dressed to kill. I wear a pair

15 of hacked-off jeans and a too-big T-shirt that I can roll up onto my head when the sun gets bad. I don't wear shoes – one, because I don't have any, and two, because you need to feel with your feet. The Mission School had a big push on getting us boots, but most of the kids sold them on. The trash is soft,

20 and our feet are hard as hooves.

Rubber is good. Just last week we got a freak delivery of old tyres from somewhere. Snapped up in minutes, they were, the men getting in first and driving us off. A half-good tyre can fetch half a dollar, and a dead tyre holds down the roof of your

25 house. [. . .] Everything turned, cleaned and bagged up – cycled down to the weighers, weighed and sold. Onto the trucks that take it back to the city, round it goes. On a good day I'll make two hundred pesos. On a bad, maybe fifty? So you live day to day and hope you don't get sick. Your life is the hook you

30 carry, there in your hand, turning the trash.

From *Trash* by ANDY MULLIGAN

Andy Mulligan
Trash

Glossary

hacked-off cut-off

Comprehension

A

1   Why is the plastic sorted into white and blue?
2   Why doesn't Raphael wear the decent clothing he finds in the trash?
3   What do you think a 'dead tyre' is? (line 24)
4   Give two reasons why the kids sold the boots the Mission School gave them.

B

1   What is the genre of this story?
2   What effect does the question in line 2 have?
3   What does the writer mean by 'a big push'? (line 18)

C

1   Why does Raphael say 'round it goes' about the rubbish after it has been sorted and bagged? (line 27)
2   What impression do you get about Raphael's life?

- Express opinions about a story
- Discuss the content and setting of a story
- Use clues in a text to answer questions

 Stretch zone

Imagine you have to write a review of the extract from *Trash*.

- How would you explain the story to your readers?
- What would you recommend about it?
- What would you say is not so good?

Be ready to share your ideas with the class.

Survey of recycling

Make two lists: one of the rubbish Raphael recycles that you also recycle at home, and another list of the rubbish he recycles that you don't.

Discuss with a partner what you find most interesting about your lists.

- Identify and discuss ideas in poems

Compare two poems about rubbish

Although the amount of rubbish we produce is widely acknowledged to be a growing problem, people have very different attitudes about whose problem it actually is. The following two poems by the same writer depict different opinions.

Not My Problem

Izzy grins, "I have my own problems"
when you start telling him yours.

Problems as pivots. Something has to turn
or move for them to dissolve.

5   You can't help thinking about trash
during hurricanes, floods, earthquakes.

Where does it all go?
How much more is born?

Wet trash is heavier than dry trash.
10   If a whole city gets devastated, what happens next?

Baghdad! Houston! San Juan! It's everyone's problem.
Don't pretend you're exempt

just because you have a big trash can and a maid.
Ha- ha, just kidding about the maid.

15   In hotel rooms, I clean up for the housekeeper
before she comes.

Trash tells its story. Who are you,
how do you spend your days.

NAOMI SHIHAB NYE

Glossary

pivot central point to turn on
exempt not required to do something

Trash Talk

Let's just throw it away.
We can get a new one.

Why recycle?
Someone's just making money off it.

5 You know that company that says
their shoes are made out of soda bottles?

Yeah right, my head is made out of peanuts.

NAOMI SHIHAB NYE

- Identify and discuss ideas in poems
- Compare two poems by the same author

Why do you think the writer chose these titles for her poems? What message is she trying to give the reader?

Comprehension

 A

1 What is 'the problem' in the first poem?

2 Does the character in the second poem believe that the shoes are made of soda bottles? Explain your answer.

 B

1 Explain why the writer says 'Wet trash is heavier than dry trash' in the first poem? (line 9)

2 Why do you think the writer says 'just because you have a big trash can and a maid' in the first poem? (line 13)

 C

1 What do the two poems have in common?

2 What is different?

3 Which poem do you prefer? Why? Give examples from the poem.

Stretch zone

What message is the writer trying to get across in these poems? Be ready to share your ideas with the class.

Writing a poem

Write a poem about rubbish and where it goes using these poems for ideas. Make sure you include lines that make people pay attention and that encourage them to think.

- Read a playscript and understand its features

A play about boys who live on the street

This scene from the play *The Garbage King* is set at a rubbish heap where children who live on the streets sift through rubbish, looking for anything valuable.

The rules of the rubbish heap

(Karate looks ill. He coughs.)

Million	Karate! Take a break.
Karate	I'm fine.
Million	Go and sit down.

(Getachew enters with Mamo and Suri.)

Learning tip

The words in italics and parentheses here are called **stage directions**. They often tell the actor what to do, how to behave, and what their tone of voice should be when they speak their lines.

5 Getachew Million! This is the guy I was telling you about.

Million *(To Getachew)* Get to work.

(Getachew goes to work on the dump.)

Million So you're Mamo.

Mamo Yes, and this is my dog, Suri.

10 *(Suri runs to the rubbish heap to play near Buffalo. Buffalo shoos her away. She growls at him and snaps at his feet.)*

Karate Here Suri!

(Suri runs to Karate. They play together.)

15 Million Getachew told me you were kidnapped.

Mamo That's right. This guy—

Million Are you a thief? *(Looks at Getachew)*

Mamo No! I'm not a thief.

Getachew I swear it was Paul who stole the chewing gum
20 from that store.

Buffalo Oh, it's not Feleke this time?

Getachew It's true!

- Read a playscript and understand its features
- Use clues in a text to answer questions
- Discuss features of the story

Million		If you join us and you steal we will beat you and then we'll kick you out. Those are the rules. *(Looks at Suri)* Your dog's too small to guard our blankets when we're away.
25		
		(Suri whines.)
Karate		I like her, Million.
Million		I guess you can train her.
30		*(Suri barks joyfully.)*
Mamo		Are you saying I'm in?
Million		You'll stay with us for a week then we'll decide. You must obey all our rules. No thieving, no fighting. Share everything. Whatever you beg or earn you bring to me. Where I say go, you go. Where I say we sleep, you sleep. OK?
35		

From *The Garbage King* by ELIZABETH LAIRD, dramatized by OLADIPO AGBOLUAJE

Comprehension

1 How can you tell Million is the gang leader?
2 What do Buffalo and Karate think of the dog, Suri?
3 What is likely to disappear when the gang are not at the rubbish heap?
4 How do you know that Million cares about Karate?

1 Why does the writer use short sentences throughout the scene? What effect does this have?
2 What sentence in the playscript shows the gang has high moral standards?
3 What punctuation shows us that Million is not interested in Mamo's past?

1 What picture do you have about the setting of the scene in the extract?
2 How do you think Mamo felt when Million explained the rules for staying in the gang?

Learning tip
It's easier to understand what's happening in a playscript if you read it out loud with different people reading the parts of the different characters.

Don't throw things away – play them!

There are many schemes for recycling our waste, from reusing glass bottles to make more bottles, to recycling plastic to make clothes and shoes. Some community projects for recycling are very inventive.

The junk orchestra: making music out of a landfill

From Paraguay's largest landfill, children in the Recycled Orchestra have inspired others across the world to create music from trash

5 "Music is the love of my life. Music has taught me so many things. It taught me to be a more disciplined person." At 18 years old, María Ríos has already outlived the dreams of all but the biggest rock'n'rollers. She has played alongside Metallica and Megadeth and in the great music halls of Europe, and she has done it all on a violin made out of rubbish.

10 A member of Paraguay's Recycled Orchestra, Ríos is confident and well-travelled. But before learning to play, she recalls the invisibility of a childhood spent amid the filth of Cateura, Asunción's largest rubbish dump.

"The people didn't pay attention to the children before. Now
15 they want to talk with us, they approach us."

In Cateura, just outside the Paraguayan capital, 40,000 people live in a desperately poor neighbourhood. Music resonates throughout the community from cheap plastic radios, yet for most residents a musical instrument is an unattainable treasure.

20 In 2006, Favio Chávez, an environmental consultant, and Nicolás "Cola" Gómez, a rubbish picker, began to wonder if they could create instruments from scraps they found on the tip face. [...]

An oil drum was a good body for a cello; a bent kitchen fork
25 for a violin tailpiece. The first few scratchy instruments were given to local kids for whom a new violin might cost a month of their parents' wages. Chávez began to train his ensemble.

"This is not a place where someone can have a violin. A violin is worth more than a house here. A violin made out of trash
30 is worth nothing, so it will not be sold or stolen," he says.

Glossary

resonates vibrates
ensemble a group

- Use clues in a text to answer questions
- Learn new vocabulary by reading different texts
- Do research for a short presentation

From their first cacophonous practice, the orchestra slowly got the hang of their idiosyncratic instruments. A short YouTube clip made to secure crowdfunding for a documentary on the children spawned hundreds of media stories from countries

35 across the world and launched them to global fame.

Now they are seasoned performers, including doing a show with heavy metal group Megadeth (who admit to being fans) and a South American tour with Metallica.

THE GUARDIAN, JULY 2015

Glossary

cacophonous inharmonious, unmusical
crowdfunding raising money for a project by collecting small amounts of money from lots of people

Comprehension

1 What caused the orchestra rapidly to become well-known around the world?
2 How did the inhabitants of Cateura usually listen to music before the orchestra was created?

1 What adjectives can you think of to describe María Ríos's life before she joined the orchestra?
2 Find out what 'idiosyncratic' means. (line 32) Why is it a good word for describing the musical instruments?

1 Apart from a fork, what other scrap materials do you think they used to make a violin?
2 Why do you think people began wanting to talk to the children when they didn't before?

Learning tip
Write new sentences using each of the Glossary words, and any other words you are unsure of, to show that you understand their meaning.

Researching decomposition

Discuss what decomposition is. Find out how long it takes for various materials to decompose:

- plastic bag
- plastic bottle
- glass bottle
- tin can
- orange peel
- leaves
- polystyrene
- paper

Present and discuss your results in class.

Read more about the boys living on a rubbish dump

The story of *Trash* continues in this extract, with Raphael telling the reader more about what he discovered at the trash heap.

The discovery

We were working together, and the bags were coming down – some of them already torn, some of them not – and that's when I found a 'special'. A special is a bag of trash, unsplit, from a rich area, and you always keep your eyes wide for one
5 of them. I can remember even now what we got ... A zucchini that was fresh enough for stew, and then a load of beaten-up tin cans. A pen, probably no good, and pens are easy to come by, and some dry papers I could stick straight in my sack – then trash and trash, like old food and a broken mirror or something,
10 and then, falling into my hand ... I know I said you don't find interesting things, but, OK – once in your life ...

It fell into my hand: a small leather bag, zipped up tight and covered in coffee-grounds. Unzipping it, I found a wallet. Next to that, a folded-up map – and inside the map, a key. Gardo
15 came right over, and we squatted there together, up on the hill. My fingers were trembling, because the wallet was fat. There were eleven hundred pesos inside, and that – let me tell you – is good money. A chicken costs one-eighty ... One hour in the video hall, twenty-five.

20 I sat there laughing ... Gardo was punching me, and I don't mind telling you, we almost danced. I gave him five hundred, which was fair because I was the one who found it. Six hundred left for me. We looked to see what else there was, but it was just a few old papers, photos, and – interesting ... an ID card.
25 A little battered and creased, but you could make him out easy enough. A man, staring up at us, right into the camera, with those frightened eyes you always have when the camera flashes. Name? José Angelico. Age? Thirty-three years old, employed as a houseboy. Unmarried and living out somewhere called
30 Green Hills – not a rich man, and that makes you sad. But what do you do? Find him in the city and say, 'Mr Angelico, sir – we'd like to return your property'?

Glossary

houseboy boy or man who works as a servant in a house

pesos unit of money used in many Latin American countries and the Philippines

zucchini (*American English*) long vegetable with dark green skin that is white inside; in British English, known as 'courgette'

Two little photos of a girl in school dress. Hard to say how old, but I reckoned seven or eight, with long dark hair and
35 beautiful eyes. Serious face, like Gardo's – as if no one had told her to smile.

We looked at the key then. It had a little tag made of yellow plastic. There was a number on both sides: 101.

The map was just a map of the city.

40 I took it all away and slipped it down my shorts – then we kept on sorting. You don't want to draw attention to yourself, or you can lose what you find. But I was excited. We were both excited, and we were right to be, because that bag changed everything. A long time later I would think to myself: *Everyone*
45 *needs a key*.

With the right key, you can bust the door wide open. Because nobody's going to open it for you.

From *Trash* by ANDY MULLIGAN

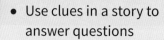

- Use clues in a story to answer questions
- Explain how language features create effects
- Be adventurous with sentences and language to create an effect

Comprehension

 A

1 Why do you think bags of trash from rich areas are better than bags from poor areas?
2 Who do you think the little girl in the photos might be?
3 What do you think the key might be for?

 B

1 What is the purpose of the dashes in lines 17 and 18?
2 Why do you think Raphael uses the word 'just' when he says the map was 'just a map of the city'? (line 39)

 C

1 Why did Raphael share the money with Gardo, even though Gardo didn't find the money?
2 Should Raphael have returned the money to Mr Angelico? Explain your answer.
3 At the end of the extract, Raphael uses a key as a symbol for something else. Explain what you think he actually means in the last two sentences.

Language tip
Symbolism describes when an object is used to stand for something else, not the literal meaning of the word. It makes writing more interesting and meaningful.

 Stretch zone

Write about a character you know from a TV programme, film or book who has found something or made a discovery. Explain how it makes the story more interesting, exciting or mysterious.

Write about an unexpected find

Write a short story in the first person about an unexpected discovery. Describe the events leading up to your discovery and what happens afterwards. Make it exciting and create a feeling of suspense. You could:

- find a mysterious box on the street
- find something unusual in an old, empty house
- make a scientific breakthrough, or something else completely different!

- Read a variety of non-fiction texts

Don't throw things away – fix them!

Landfill sites and rubbish tips are full of items that are slightly broken, or slightly worn out. Often these items are thrown away because people don't have the skills to repair the items themselves; paying to have them repaired is costly, or finding someone to repair them is too difficult. But there are alternatives. Repair Cafés are set up on the principle that repairing something is much better than throwing it away.

https://www.repaircafe.org/en/about/

What is a Repair Café?

Repair Cafés are free meeting places and they're all about repairing things (together). In the place where a Repair Café is located, you'll find tools and materials to help you make any repairs you need. On clothes, furniture, electrical appliances, bicycles, crockery, appliances, toys, et cetera. You'll also find expert volunteers, with repair skills in all kinds of fields.

Visitors bring their broken items from home. Together with the specialists, they start making their repairs in the Repair Café. It's an ongoing learning process. If you have nothing to repair, you can enjoy a cup of tea or coffee. Or you can lend a hand with someone else's repair job. You can also get inspired at the reading table – by leafing through books on repairs and DIY.

There are over 2,200 Repair Cafés worldwide. Visit one in your area or start one yourself! See also the house rules we use at the Repair Café.

Talk about …

Have you ever repaired something? If so, how did it make you feel?

Glossary

DIY stands for 'do-it-yourself' and refers to the act of making repairs to your home

Learning tip

Look out for the ways the author uses structure to organize information and help you to understand the message of the text, for example using simple questions as section headings.

- Read a variety of non-fiction texts

https://www.repaircafe.org/en/about/

Why a Repair Café?

We throw away vast amounts of stuff. Even things with almost nothing wrong, and which could get a new lease on life after a simple repair. The trouble is, lots of people have forgotten that they can repair things themselves. Especially younger generations no longer know how to do that. Knowing how to make repairs is a skill quickly lost. This is a threat to a sustainable future and to the circular economy, in which raw materials can be reused again and again.

That's why there's a Repair Café! People with repair skills get the appreciation they deserve. Invaluable practical skills are passed on. Things are being used for longer and don't have to be thrown away. This reduces the volume of raw materials and energy needed to make new products. It cuts CO_2 emissions, for example, because manufacturing new products and recycling old ones causes CO_2 to be released.

The Repair Café teaches people to see their possessions in a new light. And, once again, to appreciate their value. Repair Café volunteers also visit schools to give repair lessons. In both these ways, the Repair Café helps change people's mindset. This is essential to kindle people's enthusiasm for a sustainable society.

But most of all, the Repair Café just wants to show how much fun repairing things can be, and how easy it often is. Why don't you give it a go?

- Use clues in a text to answer questions
- Discuss the register of a text

Comprehension

A

1 Who can go to a Repair Café?

2 What will you learn at a Repair Café?

3 How are students being given the chance to learn about repairing things?

B

1 How would you describe the genre of this text?

2 Would you describe this text as formal or informal? Explain your answer with examples from the text.

3 People see their possessions in a new light when they have been repaired. What does 'in a new light' mean?

C

1 List all the benefits of Repair Cafés.

2 What do you think the atmosphere in a Repair Café would be like?

Language tip
Think about the features of **formal** and **informal language**. Which one uses contractions and which uses complex sentences, for example?

REPAIR
MEND
UPCYCLE

• Plan and proofread writing and give peer feedback

Now be a creative story writer!

Write a story about a broken object. Think about how the object broke and how it gets repaired, or even turned into something completely different. You can be as creative as you like!

Choose your genre – it could be real-life, science fiction, fantasy, or you could set it in the past. The pictures below might give you some inspiration.

Discuss your ideas with a partner and get their feedback before beginning your planning.

Make sure you check for errors and make corrections before your final draft – you can swap your rough draft with your partner.

Talk about ...

Discuss what can be done to reduce the amount of rubbish we produce on a global level.

?

How has this unit changed your attitude towards rubbish and recycling?

Plastic bottles being used as planters

A broken bowl repaired using the ancient Japanese technique of *kintsugi*, where cracks are filled with gold

Catalan architect Antoni Gaudí's famous mosaic salamander created using fragments of broken glass, tiles, and chinaware (located at the entrance to Parc Güell, Barcelona, Spain)

How can we make a difference in our communities?

> ‘It was not death or destruction
> that won that day,
> But the human courage
> Which shone more golden than
> the golden sun,
> And the human heart
> Far deeper than all the waters
> of the world.’
>
> KHUNYING CHAMNONGSRI RUTNIN

The words above are from a poem by the Thai poet Khunying Chamnongsri Rutnin. The poem was read aloud at a memorial service held on 26 December 2005 to remember the 230,000 people who died in the Indian Ocean tsunami one year before. (You read about this tsunami in Unit 5.)

Memorial services were held in all the countries affected by the tsunami. This one was held on Khao Lak beach in Thailand, and the poet's words were spoken by two schoolchildren: one English and one Thai. The English schoolgirl, Tilly Smith, was on the beach on the day of the tsunami. She knew that when the water suddenly disappeared from the beach and the shoreline retreated, a great wave would follow, because she had learned about tsunamis at school. Her warnings saved the lives of her family, and about a hundred other people.

Tilly Smith reading the poem

- Plan and draft an essay
- Think about sentence construction, punctuation and organizing your writing

The power of words

It is difficult to imagine the devastating effects of such a tragedy on the many communities affected by the 2004 tsunami. What do you think the poet's words tell us about the strength of people who are drawn together to help one another in a crisis?

How can we make a difference in our communities? Sometimes it is through the power of words. Think about this proverb from Madagascar (you looked at a proverb in Unit 6, page 82):

> ❝ **Words are like eggs: when they hatch they have wings.** ❞

When baby birds break out of their eggs, they hatch. This proverb suggests that when words are spoken, they can take on a life of their own.

Here is another proverb, from Turkey:

> ❝ **Kind words unlock an iron door.** ❞

The meaning of community

One definition of 'community' is 'sharing attitudes and interests'.

Write an essay about what community means to you. Think about the way communities are defined – sometimes by the street or the suburb in which you live, and other times by nationality or ethnic group, or shared interests. A community can be local or global. Include some of the following words in your writing:

neighbourhood

membership

citizen

group

co-operation

society

shared interests

identity

Talk about ...

- What do you think each proverb tells you about the power of words?
- What does the second proverb about kind words mean to you?
- What other proverbs can you think of? What are their meanings?

Word origins

community (n), from the Latin word *communis*, meaning 'common' or 'shared'
Related words:
- common
- communal
- commune

Learning tip
As you are planning your writing, look back to check you have included conjunctions, clauses and appropriate punctuation in order to make your writing interesting and effective.

- Write a play out of the message in a poem
- Use speech and non-verbal methods to help the audience understand the play

Why is belonging somewhere important?

Schools are communities where people often make friends, but they can also be places where some people feel left out and alone. The child in this poem remembers how it felt to move to a foreign school.

Finding a Friend

I could not speak your language
I did not know your rules.
Everything felt foreign
to an alien at school.

5   Those days are long gone now,
though I thought they'd never end.
Now I have no problems
speaking English, making friends.

Dark and haunting memories
10   of loneliness and fear,
frustration and confusion
have begun to disappear.

But one thing I'll remember,
one thing will stay the same.
15   The moment that you smiled at me
and called me by my name.

JANE CLARKE

Talk about ...

- What difficulties are experienced by the child in the poem?
- How does the child feel at first? What happened to make things change?
- What difference do you think finding a friend makes to someone who is new to the community?

Make the poem into a play

Work in small groups to write a short play based on the poem which you will perform to the rest of the class. Discuss:

- characters
- stage directions
- movement and non-verbal actions
- expression and intonation in speech
- layout of the script.

Where possible, watch some play extracts and read the playscripts for them so you can use them as a model.

What are community projects?

Sometimes people come together in an organized way to improve things in their communities and make sure that useful work gets done. Below, you will read about one such project in Staten Island, New York, USA.

An interview with Señor Juárez

The interview on the following pages is between a local newspaper reporter and Agustín Juárez, a Mexican immigrant who farms a plot of land on Staten Island. You can see the location of Zapotitlán Lagunas, where Señor Juárez comes from in Mexico, and Staten Island, New York, on the maps below.

Stretch zone

Below are some ways of saying hello in different languages.

Ahlan!	**Hallo!**
Namaste!	**Kalimera!**
Hei!	**Salud!**
Konnichiwa!	**Kia ora!**
Hola!	**Czesc!**
Jambo!	**Ciao!**
Merhaba!	

- Find out about as many of them as you can.
- Do you know this common greeting below?

السلام عليكم

- Do you know which language this is?

こんにちは

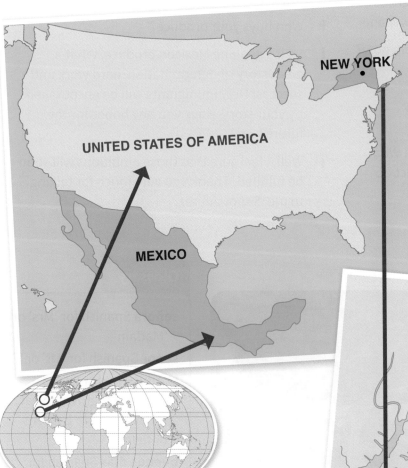

Maps showing location of Mexico, New York and Staten Island

- Understand the purpose of a text
- Organize information for an interview

Organizing an interview

The interview has been presented in a jumbled-up way. The newspaper reporter's ten questions are listed under the letters **a–j** below in the correct order. But Señor Juárez's replies are not. Can you arrange the answers, listed **1–10** on page 169, in the correct order?

Señor Juárez's first language is Spanish. The words he says in Spanish are in italics. Can you pronounce his name? Can you translate his words into your own language?

Here are the newspaper reporter's questions (in the correct order):

Learning tip
If you have to put information into a correct or better order, have a copy of each piece of information on a separate piece of paper so that you can swap the order around until you find the best way.

a Good morning, Señor Juárez. Thank you for letting me write about your experiences as a Mexican immigrant in our local newspaper.

b How long have you been in New York now?

c So you decided to emigrate?

d What was life like for you when you first arrived?

e A life-belt? A very vivid description! What exactly did the Development Project do for you?

f Was it very hard work for you?

g It's certainly an amazing market here with its 600 varieties of produce. What do you sell?

h Who buys your produce?

i So it's genuine Mexican produce. What a great story of determination, hard work and success! New immigrants will be encouraged by your story. Have you any hopes for the future?

j Well, I feel sure that those ambitions will soon be fulfilled. Thank you very much for talking to me, Señor Juárez.

A farmers' market in New York City

Glossary

señora Spanish for 'Mrs' or 'Madam'

señor Spanish for 'Mr' or 'Sir'

produce (n) fruits and vegetables grown to eat, for example, in gardens or fields

buenos días Spanish for 'hello' or 'good day'

encantado polite way to greet a stranger in Spanish, like the English phrase 'Pleased to meet you'

adiós Spanish for 'goodbye'

sí Spanish for 'yes'

- Understand the purpose of a text
- Organize information for an interview

1 I came here seven years ago from Mexico. I grew up in a place in southern Mexico called Zapotitlán Lagunas. Ah, those were happy times in my native country, but hard times, too. I left school to help my father and my brothers on our farm, but however hard we worked, we never had enough money.

2 *Buenos días, señora. Encantado.* If your article gives hope to immigrants like me, I am happy to talk to you.

3 You're welcome, *señora. Adiós.*

4 It was hard for me. My English was not good. I wasn't used to a big city and I missed my family. I was lonely. But I was lucky. Very lucky. I was told about a community project in New York which helped immigrant farmers like me. It was called the New Farmer Development Project and to me it was as though I was drowning and someone threw me … what do they call those rubber rings to save a drowning man?

5 It was a difficult decision. But yes, our family decided that because I was the eldest son, I should emigrate to New York.

6 *Sí, sí.* Oh yes, it was hard work. It's still hard work, but now I have some of my family to help me. I work 60 hours a week in the kitchens of 'Antonio'. It's an Italian restaurant on Staten Island. But my heart isn't in the kitchens! My heart is on my farm with my plants. Every hour God gives me, I am digging, planting, watering, weeding, sowing, harvesting … Each week we come here to St George Greenmarket to sell our produce.

7 Indeed yes! Just this. A piece of land of my own. And a tractor!

8 The people there gave me the gift of a new life. The project owns Decker Farm on Staten Island and they gave me a plot of land there, 5,000 square metres.

9 After two years on Staten Island, I bought an old van and each week we load it up with *alache, epazote, pipicha, tomatillos,* lettuce, beans and much more, and come over on the ferry to New York City to the market here.

10 Mexicans! Mexicans love their traditional dishes and remedies. I come here and in an hour all my produce has gone! They all know me now and my chillies are the hottest in the market. I joke and say, "Taste one! If it's not hot enough for you, don't buy!" They always buy! That's because my seeds are the real thing – they come from Mexico.

Glossary

alache green-leaf plant used in Mexican soup

epazote herb used for stomach pains

pipicha spicy herb used in tacos

tomatillos small round green fruit used in Mexican dishes such as salsa

Comprehension

A

1 Describe what life was like in the community that Señor Juárez came from in Mexico.

B

1 Give three examples of facts and three examples of opinions in Señor Juárez's answers.

C

1 How successful do you think the community project that helped Señor Juárez is? Give evidence from the text to support your answer.

- Read a range of texts and express opinions

Mexican food is full of fruits, vegetables and herbs!

- *Alache* is a green-leaf plant essential for Mexican vegetable soup.
- *Tomatillos* are used for salsa verde.
- The fruit of the prickly pear cactus is used to make a delicious ice cream.
- *Epazote* is a herb used to ease stomach pains.
- *Pipicha* is a spicy herb used in tacos.
- Avocados are the creamy fruit used to make guacamole.
- Habanero chillies are often used in Mexican dishes to add heat and flavour.

Prickly pear fruit

Epazote

Tomatillos: Mexican green tomatoes

Calabaza en Tacha is a traditional Mexican dessert

Salsa verde with tortilla chips

Ingredients for a tasty guacamole

Mexican tacos, made using tortilla flatbreads

Habanero chilli

Chocolate and the beans it is made from

Mexican food quiz

Share your knowledge about Mexican food, then use the information on page 170 about Mexican fruits, vegetables and herbs, plus your own general knowledge and online research to answer the fun quiz below about Mexican food!

Quiz

1 Look at the picture on the previous page. What do you think the main ingredients are in the traditional Mexican dessert *Calabaza en Tacha*?

2 What different colours of corn tortillas chips can you get?

3 What is another name for 'tuna fruit'?

4 What do you fill tortillas with?

5 Are tacos hard or soft?

6 Chocolate originated in Mexico, but what plant does it come from?

7 What is another name for the Mexican husk tomato?

8 What herb is also know as 'stinky weed' or 'Mexican tea'?

Foods from different communities

In the interview with Señor Juárez, we hear how the Mexican immigrants in New York want to buy Señor Juárez's produce to make their favourite Mexican dishes. Countries all over the world have their own traditional dishes. What is your favourite dish?

- Research a favourite dish, either from your own community or from another one anywhere in the world.
- Write an information text about the community or region it comes from, why the meal is important to the people, and why certain ingredients are used.
- Include a list of ingredients. Is there a special sauce? A special mixture of herbs? A special way of cooking the dish?
- Add a photograph of the dish if you can.

Tavče gravče (pronounced 'tav-cheh grav-cheh'), a traditional Macedonian dish of beans baked in an earthenware pot with red peppers and onions

- Read a range of texts and express opinions

Read about an isolated community

The Inuit people have lived and thrived in the Arctic for thousands of years.

There are in excess of 64,000 Inuits living in Canada, in 53 communities across the northern regions of the country, mostly along the Arctic coast.

Inuit communitities

Both community and family have always been very important to the Inuit. The Inuit language is made up of
5 a variety of dialects that vary from region to region. More than half of the Inuit speak a dialect called Inuktitut.

The Inuit live in a challenging
10 climate. There are few materials to be found on their land for building as no trees grow. Wood and other materials have to be brought in from outside. Traditionally, Inuit communities live in homes made from snow blocks known as igloos in
15 winter, and in summer they stretch animal skins around a frame. During the twentieth century, the Inuit began to move into towns for work where healthcare and schools are available, although for many years the children were not allowed to speak their own language at school.

20 The arrival of explorers and traders threatened the Inuit way of life but they have managed to keep their culture and traditions, such as singing, dancing and story-telling and today, community elders are still held in high regard, holding important
25 positions in the community.

Due to the remoteness of the communities, fresh food and other consumable items have to be brought in by plane. Unfortunately, the abiltity of planes to do this is dependent on the weather
30 being suitable for them to land, which means deliveries cannot be guaranteed all year round,

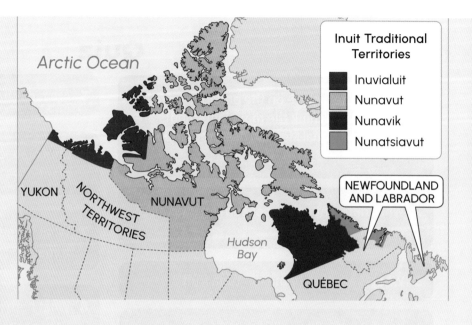

Arctic Ocean

Inuit Traditional Territories
- Inuvialuit
- Nunavut
- Nunavik
- Nunatsiavut

YUKON
NORTHWEST TERRITORIES
NUNAVUT

NEWFOUNDLAND AND LABRADOR

Hudson Bay

QUÉBEC

An Inuit family

- Prepare and give an interesting presentation using suitable visual aids
- Write and speak in a suitable style for the task

and food is expensive when it is available. The Inuit have always hunted for food, but younger people are not as interested
35 as they were in learning hunting skills and prefer to rely on the imported food, thereby risking losing one of their community's famous traditions.

Comprehension

 A

1 What benefits are there for the Inuit to living in towns?
2 Why do you think younger Inuit people prefer to get their food from shops?

 B

1 What is the purpose of this text?
2 What does 'held in high regard' mean? (paragraph 3)

 C

1 Why do you think Inuit children were not allowed to speak the Inuit language at school?
2 What effect would this have had on their culture and sense of community?

?

Do you think remote communities are better off if they are kept away from the outside world?

Give a presentation about an isolated community

Do research on another community that is largely isolated from the outside world due to its location. This might be due to weather, physical boundaries (such as mountains or forests), or because they live on an island far from the mainland. Find photographs, video clips and examples of the art, music or literature from your chosen community. Present your findings to the rest of the class.

A story about a doctor who talks to animals

Doctor Dolittle, a human doctor who can speak to animals, decides to focus on treating animals instead. Animals who are sick come to his house and most of them like it so much that they never want to leave. Doctor Dolittle is so kind-hearted that he lets them stay, and they form an unusual community in his house, which is full to the brim. This extract shows how the doctor's kindness starts to cause him financial problems, and how the animals come together to help him for the good of their community and to repay his generosity.

The animals do their bit

Some of the animals who came to see him were so sick that they had to stay at the Doctor's house for a week. And when they were getting better they used
5 to sit in chairs on the lawn. And often even after they got well, they did not want to go away – they liked the Doctor and his house so much. And he never had the heart to refuse them when they
10 asked if they could stay with him. So in this way he went on getting more and more pets.

And another time, when the circus came to Puddleby, the crocodile who had a
15 bad toothache escaped at night and came into the Doctor's garden. The Doctor talked to him in crocodile-language and took him into the house and made his tooth better. But when the crocodile saw what a nice house it was – with all the different places for the different kinds of animals – he too
20 wanted to live with the Doctor. When the circus-men came to take him back he got so wild and savage that he frightened them away. But to every one in the house he was always as gentle as a kitten.

With all these mouths to fill, and the house to look after, and
25 no one to do the mending, and no money coming in to pay the butcher's bill, things began to look very difficult. But the Doctor didn't worry at all. "Money is a nuisance," he used to say. "We'd all be much better off if it had never been invented. What does money matter, so long as we are happy?"

- Use clues in a story to answer questions
- Explain how language features create effects

30 But soon the animals themselves began to get worried. And one evening when the Doctor was asleep in his chair before the kitchen-fire they began talking it over among themselves in whispers. And the owl, Too-Too, who was good at arithmetic, figured it out that there was only money enough left to last

35 another week – if they each had one meal a day and no more. Then the parrot said, "I think we all ought to do the housework ourselves. At least we can do that much. After all, it is for our sakes that the old man finds himself so lonely and so poor." So it was agreed that the monkey, Chee-Chee, was to do the

40 cooking and mending; the dog was to sweep the floors; the duck was to dust and make the beds; the owl, Too-Too, was to keep the accounts … They made Polynesia, the parrot, housekeeper and laundress, because she was the oldest.

Of course at first they all found their new jobs very hard to do

45 – all except Chee-Chee, who had hands … But they soon got used to it; and they used to think it great fun to watch Jip, the dog, sweeping his tail over the floor with a rag tied onto it for a broom. After a little they got to do the work so well that the Doctor said that he had never had his house kept so tidy or so

50 clean before.

From *The Story of Doctor Dolittle* by HUGH LOFTING

Language tip
Anthropomorphism means giving human characteristics to non-humans, such as animals. With a partner, find examples in this extract.

Comprehension

A

1 What is Doctor Dolittle's opinion of money?
2 What do the animals like about staying at Doctor Dolittle's house?

B

1 Find three auxiliary verbs in the extract. Write out the phrases they are found in.
2 In the second paragraph the writer uses a simile: 'as gentle as a kitten'. What does this tell you about how the crocodile has settled into the animal community at the house?

C

1 Why do you think sick people stop coming to visit Doctor Dolittle?
2 If you could talk to any animal, which type of animal would it be? Explain your answer.
3 How might the world be different if we could talk with animals?

How can we best work together?

The cartoon pictures below have something to teach us about communities. Look at the pictures of the donkeys with a partner. You can see that they are tied together.

Talk about ...

- What are the donkeys doing in each picture?
- What problem do the donkeys have?
- How do they solve it?
- What do you think these donkeys can teach us about solving a problem in our community?

Working together

Individuals can attend meetings, help their neighbours, support charity events and volunteer their time, but if people with common goals work together as a community, they will have more influence over things that happen locally, and communities can have a say in the big decisions that affect their lives.

Not everyone feels they can take part though. Discuss why some people might be left out of a community group. How can we make sure that everyone is included?

Writing a newsletter to a community group

Groups of people often organize events in their community. This might be a street party, or a carnival to raise money, and usually involves people enjoying themselves and getting to know one another.

Plan and write a newsletter to be distributed locally and on social media encouraging members of your local community to help with an event of your choice.

Pick vocabulary that will encourage people to get involved, such as: 'support', 'helpful', 'successful'. Check your work for any spelling errors.

Make sure your local community takes care of everyone.

- Plan and write a community newsletter
- Proofread and check for errors
- Look at words with prefixes and suffixes
- Develop strategies to help you with difficult spellings

Learning tip
If you have trouble remembering how to spell the same words, write them on pieces of paper and stick them around your house so that you see them many times during the day.

Stretch zone

Find out what the following prefixes and suffixes mean: *anti-, auto-, inter-, trans-, -ment, -ness.*

For example, the prefix *mis-* means 'bad' ('lead' means 'to show someone the right way, so 'mislead' means to give someone the wrong idea).

12 Courage

What does courage look like?

> ❝ Courage isn't having the strength to go on – it is going on when you don't have strength. ❞
>
> NAPOLÉON BONAPARTE

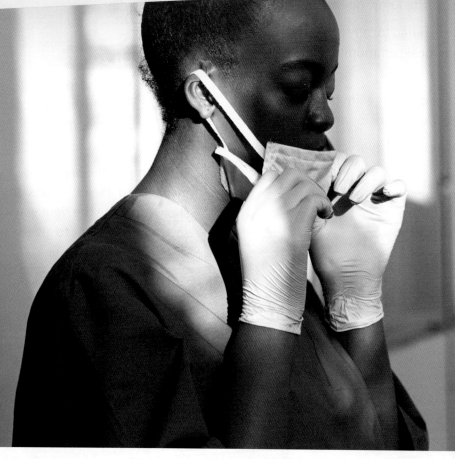

Talk about ...

- What does courage mean to you?
- When have you been courageous?
- Who are the most courageous people in the town or city where you live?

A dictionary definition of courage would be the ability to do something dangerous, or to face pain or opposition, without showing fear. But what does courage look like in real life? Courageous people do things and say things even when it is difficult or dangerous for them and there are many examples from history and in everyday life that we might see in news reports on television, or which happen behind the scenes and are uncelebrated. You will be learning about a few of these courageous people throughout this unit.

Word origins

courage (n), from the Latin word *cor*, meaning 'heart'
Related words:
- courageous
- encourage
- encouragement

- Read a variety of texts and consider their features

Read a story about a courageous boy

Iqbal is a fictional story based on true events. The story tells how Iqbal arrives at a carpet factory where children are forced to work, and how he convinces the other children that they must be responsible for their own escape or remain slaves forever. In this extract, Iqbal has been locked up by the boss as a punishment for cutting up a carpet.

Chapter 6

"Iqbal," I called quietly. "Iqbal!"

From his deep pockets, Karim brought out a box of matches. We could see Iqbal in the flickering light of the match. He forced himself up from the corner where he was crouching and
5 came towards us. His lips were split from thirst and the flame of the match bothered his eyes.

The cistern that we called the Tomb was wide, but so low that anyone standing could touch the grating with the tips of his fingers. I passed the small bottle through the bars to Iqbal. He
10 drank avidly and then poured the rest over his poor face.

His throat was too dry to let him talk to us, and although we had a million questions to ask him, we couldn't think of anything to say.

15 The sight of him suffering moved and confused me. And I remembered that this was only his first day in the Tomb. Salman was nervous. Karim behaved as if he was just passing by and had nothing to do with anything. Ali pushed his hand through the bars and took Iqbal's hand.

"Hold on," he said. "We're here now."

20 "Yes," I said, "we'll come back every night."

"I have to admit you're pretty brave," said Salman.

"The hell we'll return," said Karim. "I'm not about to risk anything."

"Thanks, friends," croaked Iqbal. His voice was like a thin wire.

25 We went back every night.

Chapter 7

Iqbal was released from the Tomb three days later. When we saw him walk across the courtyard on wobbly legs, blinded by the light, his arms covered with angry insect bites, we pitied him, but we were proud, too. We would have liked to cheer
30 and applaud, but Hussain's grim eyes warned us to keep quiet. The master gave Iqbal a day and a night to rest, and we held back our curiosity and respected his fitful sleep. We took turns watching over him and soothing his pain by sponging him with cool water. We could see that Iqbal would recover quickly,
35 thanks to our nightly visits, the food, the water, and those oranges that Ali had stolen from the garden for him.

"Brother," said Salman one morning when Iqbal finally returned to work, "you were really strong. Nobody has ever had the courage to do something like that to Hussain Khan. Do you
40 realize how angry he still is about the carpet? But you were also foolish. What have you gained by destroying the carpet? Three days in the Tomb, that's all."

"You all took risks, coming out at night to help me," Iqbal replied. "If the master had discovered you, what would you
45 have gotten out of it?"

"What has that got to do with anything?" asked Salman. "We did it for you."

> **Language tip**
> **Modal verbs**, such as 'could', 'can't', 'should' and 'must', show the likelihood of something happening.
> For example:
> 'We <u>could</u> see that Iqbal would recover quickly.'
> 'There <u>must</u> be someone.'

> **Glossary**
>
> **loom** machine for making cloth

- Read a variety of texts and consider their features

"Well," said Iqbal, "and I did it for you, in a certain sense, as well as for me."

50 "What do you mean?" I asked.

"It means that this kind of life isn't right. We should return to our families; we shouldn't be chained to our looms and forced to work like slaves."

"I'd like to go home, too," I said, "but we can't."

55 "Why not?"

"Because ... because ...," burst in Salman, "because the master is stronger than us. Because it's always been like this. Because nobody cares about us."

"We'll find somebody to help us. Out there. There must
60 be someone."

"Out there? What's going on in your head?"

"I don't know," said Iqbal.

"You got too much heat down in the Tomb, brother." Salman shook his head. "Everybody's too scared here."

65 "That's not true." Iqbal laughed. "You're not afraid anymore. Neither are Fatima and little Ali."

A carpet factory in Pakistan

"I'm not afraid of anybody!" declared Ali, hiding behind my skirt.

"Even Karim is less frightened than before. Isn't that true?"

70 "Don't drag me into your dumb plans," hissed Karim, "and remember anyway, I'm not afraid of anything."

"Not even Hussain?"

"I'm not scared of him," Karim assured us. "I respect him. It's different."

75 "I think the others are less frightened, too," Iqbal said.

"Back in line! Back in line!" yelled Karim, as he glimpsed the figure of the mistress crossing the courtyard.

From *Iqbal* by FRANCESCO D'ADAMO

- Use evidence from a text to answer questions
- Explain the effect of language features used by the writer

Comprehension

A

1 What did the children do to help Iqbal when he was in the Tomb?

2 What did they do to help him after he was let out?

3 Ali said he wasn't afraid of anyone. What do you think and why?

B

1 Find a simile in Chapter 6. What picture does it give you?

2 What is the difference between respecting someone and being scared of them? (lines 73–74)

3 The children call each other 'brother'. Why do you think they do this?

C

1 Do you think Iqbal was brave or foolish to have ripped up a carpet in protest to Hussain Khan?

2 What can you learn from Iqbal?

Language tip
Remember: a **simile** likens one thing to another, usually by using the words 'like' or 'as'.
For example:
'Her eyes shone <u>like</u> diamonds.'
'Joe was <u>as</u> clever <u>as</u> a fox.'

Writing a biography

Use these facts about Iqbal Masih to write a biography of his life:

- Aged four – sent to a carpet factory to repay his father's debt of around US$12
- Worked twelve hours/day, tied to his loom
- Was half normal size due to lack of food and exercise
- Escaped aged ten, began to speak out against child slavery
- 1994 – Iqbal awarded Reebok Human Rights Youth in Action Award
- 16 April 1995 – Iqbal murdered, aged twelve.

Find out more information about Iqbal Masih to make your biography more detailed.

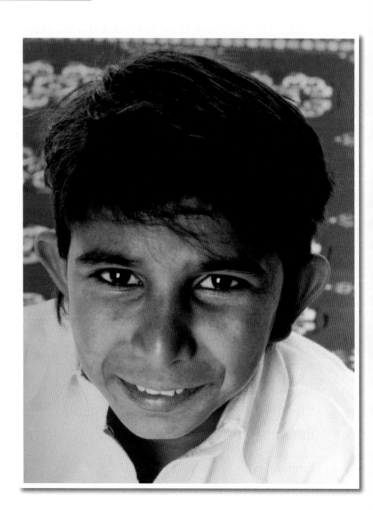

A magazine article about a tsunami survivor

On 26 December in 2004, an earthquake struck beneath the Indian Ocean, triggering a tsunami that killed more than 230,000 people in fourteen countries. You have already read about this tragedy in earlier units. The following extract is taken from an article published in *The Guardian* newspaper on 15 November 2014 and describes the experience of Edie Fassnidge, who lost both her mother and sister in the tsunami in Thailand. After surviving the tsunami, she managed to swim to some rocks.

Glossary

freak *(of an event or the weather)* very unusual and unexpected

headland narrow piece of high land that sticks out from the coast into the sea

adrenaline substance produced in the body when you are excited, afraid or angry

Surviving the tsunami

Alone on the rocks, she considered her chances of being rescued. At that stage, she had no idea of the scale of what had just happened – she assumed the tsunami had just been a freak, local wave and that a search party would be along soon. But she also
5   realised that she was very isolated. There was no way to dry land except via the sea, and since she was now terrified of the water, she started climbing up the rocky headland. "Before long I was climbing through really dense, spiky gorse bushes, pulling myself up through branches; I could feel myself getting cut even more. It was getting steeper and steeper, and I realised that
10 it wasn't going to work. I needed to turn back and preserve my energy."

On climbing down, she was suddenly surrounded by large, orangey-brown ants. "I felt them first in my feet, which were really cut up; it was as if something was biting into the core of my body, electric pain, like an electric shock, and they swarmed all over me." There were too many to pick off,
15 and this was the first time that she cried. "I got really angry and I screamed, 'Why is this happening to me?'" She moved down to the water, heard a helicopter, and motioned to it, shouting. It was flying low, but didn't slow down, just kept moving on out to sea. There was no option but to follow it, to do what she was dreading: she lowered herself back into the water.

20 Fassnidge swam against the currents, then rested, aware of how close she might be to dying if she didn't get help. "I was feeling drained and out of energy, out of ideas. I lay down and gave myself a bit of a talking to, told myself that if I didn't do anything, I could die." Finally she saw a small gap between some rocks and decided to squeeze through. She emerged on to a
35 small, rocky beach. After so long without water she knew she was running solely on adrenaline, but she crawled, walked and paddled as far as she could, finally turning a corner and seeing two men next to some boats. A paramedic arrived and she was carried to a beach; she hadn't spoken for hours, but her story began tumbling out.

THE GUARDIAN, 15 November 2014

- Explore how setting and character are developed
- Explain how language features create effects

Comprehension

A 👤

1 What did Edie waste energy doing?

2 What made Edie cry?

3 What did Edie say to herself to give her the will to carry on?

B 👤

1 Strong verbs can create a more dramatic and traumatic effect. Explain what effect these verbs have on how the reader understands the scene: 'terrified' (line 6), 'swarmed' (line 14), 'tumbling out' (line 39).

2 Why did the writer use the three verbs 'crawled', 'walked' and 'paddled' to describe how Edie made her way along the beach at the end of the extract?

C 👥

1 Why do you think Edie was scared of getting back into the water?

2 How do you think she felt when the helicopter didn't slow down?

Talk about ...

Discuss with a partner what you learn about Edie's character in the extract. Be ready to share your thoughts with your teacher and the rest of the class.

Devastation left by the tsunami

184

Read a poem about facing your fears

We are often in a better position to face our fears if we have someone we trust beside us, to hold our hand, or whose presence just reassures us. To children, sticking with a parent or a trusted adult is usually the sensible strategy in the middle of the night, even if they are brave, as this poem reveals.

- Read a wide range of poems
- Identify and discuss ideas in poems

Being Brave at Night

The other night 'bout two o'clock, or maybe it was three,
An elephant with shining tusks came chasing after me.
His trunk was wavin' in the air an' spoutin' jets of steam
An' he was out to eat me up, but still I didn't scream
5   Or let him see that I was scared – a better thought I had,
I just escaped from where I was and crawled in bed with Dad.

One time there was a giant who was horrible to see,
He had three heads and twenty arms, an' he came after me
And red hot fire came from his mouths and every hand was red
10 And he declared he'd grind my bones and make them into bread.
But I was just too smart for him, I fooled him mighty bad,
Before his hands could collar me I crawled in bed with Dad.

I ain't scared of nothin' that comes pesterin' me at night.
Once I was chased by forty ghosts all shimmery an' white.
15 An' I just raced 'em round the room an' let 'em think maybe
I'd have to stop an' rest awhile, when they could capture me.
Then when they leapt onto my bed, Oh Gee! But they were mad
To find that I had slipped away an' crawled in bed with Dad.

No giants, ghosts or elephants have dared to come in there
20 'Coz if they did he'd beat 'em up and chase 'em to their lair.
They just hang 'round the children's rooms
an' snap an' snarl an' bite
An' laugh if they can make 'em yell
for help with all their might.
25 But I don't ever yell out loud. I'm not that sort of lad,
I slip from out the covers and I crawl in bed with Dad.

EDGAR ALBERT GUEST

- Identify and discuss ideas in a poem
- Discuss how language features create effects
- Use a suitable style of English for the purpose of writing

Comprehension

1 Who was annoyed?
2 What is the child scared of?
3 Who will protect the child?

1 Is the poem written in Standard or Non-Standard English? Give reasons for your answer.
2 What does 'he was out to' mean? (line 4)
3 What does 'collar me' mean? (line 12)
4 Find an example of alliteration in the poem.
5 Find an example of a metaphor.
6 What effect do all the contracted words have in the poem?

1 How courageous is the child in the poem? Use evidence from the poem to support your answer.
2 How would you describe the child's imagination? Use evidence from the poem to support your answer.

Language tip
Remember: a **metaphor** says something **is** something else.

Stretch zone
Find out what hyperbole means. There are some examples of it in the poem. Can you find them?

Standard English and Non-Standard English

Non-Standard English can include slang, local dialects, incorrect spellings and contracted words and is used in everyday situations, whereas **Standard English** includes correct grammar, punctuation and spelling.

- Create a table with two columns. In the first column, write the heading 'Standard English', and in the second column, write the heading 'Non-Standard English'.
- Under each heading, list the features of Standard English and Non-Standard English.
- Look back through this unit and any other formal or informal texts you have studied. Add examples of Standard English and Non-Standard English to your table to illustrate the features you have identified.

- Read a wide range of stories
- Discuss the context and setting of a story

The spark of courage

Eliza is a working-class girl in nineteenth-century London. She is angry because her family and friends work long hours yet never have enough money to live on, and because conditions at the matchstick factory where she and her sister work are so harsh. She is angry that no one seems to care. When Eliza speaks out, her words spark fury among the rest of the workers and the flame of rebellion is lit. She helps organize a protest rally in Hyde Park, London. Mrs Billingham is a wealthy lady who believes in social justice and fairness.

Lightning Strike

"They need to hear it from one of us," I said to Nell.

"They need to hear it from you," she said.

"Me?" I said.

5 "Ain't you the girl who told Mr Fettler where he could stick his job?" said Mary, who was standing on the other side of Nell.

And the next thing I knew I was up on the platform.

I don't know how I got there. I think it was Mary and Sally who pushed me up. One minute I was amongst the crowd, the next I was looking down on them.

10 And I didn't have a single clue of what to say.

Mrs Billingham had stood aside and was waiting for me to begin. I gawped like a fish out of water for what seemed like an eternity. I looked at that crowd. All those faces.

Match girls. Strangers. Because it wasn't just us. It was them
15 too. I could see toffs. And I could hear their thoughts as clearly as if they'd shouted them aloud.

Ugly, common creature!

Vulgar little thing!

There was a man in a top hat looking at me like I was nothing.
20 I don't think it was the same man who'd laughed at me and Nell that Saturday night, but he was cut from the very same cloth.

But there were other people in that crowd who were egging me on. Old Ma Lambert. Sally. Jen. Mary. Nell. The faces of

Glossary

match girls women who worked in the matchstick factories in nineteenth-century London

toff (*informal*) disapproving way of talking about somebody from a high social class

vulgar not having or showing good taste; not polite, pleasant or well-behaved

egg on (*informal*) encourage somebody to do something

187

- Read a wide range of stories
- Discuss the context and setting of a story

25 neighbours. Friends. People who struggled to get by. I was doing this for them. For us.

So I started speaking.

"Mrs Billingham – bless her!" I said. "She wants to help us and don't think I'm not grateful for that because I am. But all of us here know Mrs Billingham can go home at the end of the day 30 and she can have a nice big dinner and climb into a nice warm bed. She can shut her eyes at night and she won't have to lie there on a hard floor, listening to her belly rumbling and beetles scuttling up the wall. She doesn't have to live it, not like I do. I live it every single day, and I can tell you God's honest truth.

35 "The newspaper said our minds have been turned by the Socialists," I went on. "That we've been led astray.

"That's a bunch of lies. We're here because we want to be. Mrs Billingham didn't start this. I did. Me and my sister walked out and the rest of the girls followed. We did it of our own 40 accord. And you know why? Because we've had enough.

"We've had enough of being bullied by a thieving foreman. We've had enough of having our wages docked for no reason. We've had enough of seeing our mothers, our sisters and our friends die of phossy jaw. We've had enough of the boss lying 45 about it, saying it doesn't exist. We've had enough of being terrified every minute of every day that we'll be next, and being scared witless every time one of us gets a toothache.

"Some of you are looking at me and seeing a skinny little match girl. You're wondering who the hell I think I am, getting up 50 here and daring to talk to you lot? I can see you thinking it, over there, missus. Yes – you in the purple dress with your arms folded. You think I should stay in my place, don't you? And you, sir." I pointed to the toff. "Standing there in your top hat ... thinking I'm a scruffy little urchin with no right to be here. 55 I've got a flaming nerve, haven't I?

"Well, you're right, sir," I continued. "I have got a flaming nerve. And so has every single match girl in the factory. We've all got hearts and minds and souls that are just as good as yours. And we are standing up for ourselves. We are going to 60 yell from the rooftops until everyone in this city hears us. We

Glossary

Socialists political group fighting for a more equal economic system

phossy jaw bone cancer caused by contact with phosphorus, a poisonous chemical used in match making in the nineteenth and early twentieth centuries

urchin (*old-fashioned*) young child who is poor and dirty

?

Why do you think we need courage to stand up for what we believe to be right? What might people be afraid of?

demand to be treated fair. And this time, this time we will succeed. We will win this.

"I'm just one person. What can one person do, eh? Well, maybe one person can't do much, no more than one drop of water
65 can be a flood. But if there are hundreds, thousands of drops all joining together? Then you get a river as big as the Thames. And we all know that when the tide turns, there's nothing on earth that can resist that river. As long as we stay united in this struggle, we will be unstoppable.

70 "Who's with us?" I finished.

Judging from the cheering and the roaring, everyone in Hyde Park was. All apart from the toff, who turned on his heel and left.

From *Lightning Strike* by TANYA LANDMAN

189

- Use clues in a story to answer questions
- Write from a character's point of view
- Write a newspaper report using suitable vocabulary and features

Comprehension

 A

1 What sort of people attended the rally?
2 What differences were there between Eliza's life and Mrs Billingham's?
3 What clues are there in the extract that it was mainly girls and women, not men, who worked in the matchstick factories? Give quotes from the extract to support your answer.

 B

1 Explain what 'cut from the very same cloth' means. (line 21)
2 Find some examples of Non-Standard English in the extract.

 C

1 What inspired Eliza to protest against conditions in the matchstick factories?
2 How do you think Eliza's life would be different today?

 Stretch zone

Think of a cause that you think is worth campaigning for. What could you do to raise awareness and carry out a successful campaign?

Be a news reporter

While Eliza is a fictional character, the match girls really did go on strike in 1888 in London. Imagine you are a newspaper reporter attending the rally in Hyde Park. You heard Eliza's speech and saw how different people in the crowd responded.

- Think about the key features of a newspaper report first.
- Whose side are you going to take in your newspaper article? Will your writing show a bias towards one side or the other?
- Will you include quotes?
- Are you going to speak to anyone who was in the crowd?

Discuss your plans with a partner before writing.

- Read a wide range of texts
- Give your own opinions clearly and confidently

Read the diary of the great explorer Scott of the Antarctic

The following extract is taken from Captain Robert Falcon Scott's diary and was written on either 16 or 17 March 1912. This entry describes the last days of the Antarctic explorer's failed expedition to be the first to reach the South Pole.

Friday, March 16 or Saturday 17 – Lost track of dates, but think the last correct. Tragedy all along the line. At lunch, the day before yesterday, poor Titus Oates said he couldn't go on; he proposed we should leave him in his
5   sleeping-bag. That we could not do, and we induced him to come on, on the afternoon march. In spite of its awful nature for him he struggled on and we made a few miles. At night he was worse and we knew the end had come.

10   Should this be found I want these facts recorded. Oates's last thoughts were of his Mother, but immediately before he took pride in thinking that his regiment would be pleased with the bold way in which he
15   met his death. We can testify to his bravery. He has borne intense suffering for weeks without complaint, and to the very last was able and willing to discuss outside subjects. He did not – would
20   not – give up hope till the very end. He was a brave soul. This was the end. He slept through the night before last, hoping not to wake; but he woke in the morning – yesterday. It was
25   blowing a blizzard. He said, "I am just going outside and may be some time." He went out into the blizzard and we have not seen him since.

?

Discuss whether you think explorers could get into this situation today.

- Use clues in a text to answer questions
- Discuss the context and setting of a story
- Write a diary

Comprehension

 A

1 What were the last two things in Oates's thoughts?
2 How long had Oates been experiencing difficulty?

 B

1 What is the type of register used in this diary entry?
2 What is Scott implying when he writes 'Should this be found'? (line 10)

 C

1 Why do you think Scott lost track of the date?
2 Why didn't Scott and his team want to leave Oates in his sleeping bag?
3 In what way was Oates particularly courageous?

 Stretch zone

Find out about Scott's Antarctic expedition and report back to the class with your findings.

Now it's your turn to write a diary

Talk about the features you find in a diary. Imagine you are in a situation that needs you to have courage, such as being lost in a snowy climate. Now write a diary entry of your own, explaining your actions and your feelings about being lost. How long is the danger going to last? Do you find your way out or are you rescued?